Dear Dottie,
Enjoy this book!

Love,
Margie

Child of Pain Children of Joy

Child of Pain Children of Joy

Ike Keay
with William Deerfield

Fleming H. Revell Company
Old Tappan, New Jersey

Scripture quotations identified KJV are from the King James Version of the Bible.
Scripture quotations identified NAS are from the New American Standard Bible, © The Lockman Foundation 1960, 1962, 1963, 1968, 1971, 1972, 1973, 1975, 1977.
Scripture quotations marked NIV are from the Holy Bible, New International Version. Copyright © 1973, 1978, 1984 International Bible Society. Used by permission of Zondervan Bible Publishers.
Quotation from *Chattanooga News–Free Press* used by permission.
In order to protect privacy, certain names of persons and locales have been changed.

Library of Congress Cataloging-in-Publication Data

Keay, Ike.
Child of pain, children of joy.

1. Church work with children of prisoners—Tennessee. 2. Bethel Bible Village. 3. Keay, Ike. I. Deerfield, William. II. Title.
BV4464.2.K43 1989 259′.5 89-8368
ISBN 0-8007-1620-5

Published by the Fleming H. Revell Company
Old Tappan, New Jersey 07675
Printed in the United States of America

TO the most important people of my life:
Johanna Christina Smith Keay
loving Christian mother
and
Carolyn Jane Conrad Keay
loving Christian wife and mother
and
our four special gifts from God:
Kim, Debbie, Brian, and Alan
and
Praise to our wonderful God who made all this possible.

Contents

Part Three "Suffer the Little Children. . . ."

Foreword

Can it be ten years ago that I first heard about Ike Keay and Bethel Bible Village? (Time *does* fly, doesn't it?) I remember my brother Nick called me to ask if I would host a charity golf tournament for some children's home in Chattanooga, run by a guy with a colorful name: Ike Keay (Kay). For your information, it's the only children's home in the United States exclusively for prisoners' children.

Despite my crowded schedule I reluctantly agreed, thinking it would be a one-shot deal. Was I ever wrong! I got hooked by Ike, Bethel, and the beautiful bunch of kids Ike takes care of.

And I'm not alone. The same thing has since happened to my wife, Shirley, my daughter Debby . . . and actors Fred MacMurray and wife June Haver . . . *and* Perry Como . . . *and* B. J. Thomas . . . *and* Sandi Patti . . . *and* Glen Campbell, plus a host of other entertainers, Christian, pop, and country, from every part of the music industry.

I've been returning each year for ten years now, for what has become the Pat Boone Bethel Celebrity Spectacular, playing golf (of course) and hosting a celebrity picnic with the kids, a big concert, and the awards banquet on a long, festive weekend in May, during which each year more entertainers and athletes get "hooked" on Bethel and its ministry to the hurting children of prisoners.

I've already told Ike and Carolyn Keay they'll have to beat me with a stick to keep me from being there each year. My hope is that we'll finally get that whole Spectacular weekend on national television, so that America can be made aware of what goes on in this idyllic, magic place called Bethel.

I had heard most of the story contained in this book. I've grilled Ike and Carolyn through the years about what led them to Bethel, what the forces were that created the deep and obvious commitment they have to young children—children society has ignored—and how Bethel Bible Village in its quiet glory came to be. But even though each year they've shared a bit more of the story with me, I still found some surprises in this magnificent narrative.

When I started reading an early manuscript of *Child of Pain, Children of Joy,* I couldn't quit and read it straight through from beginning to end. I have a hunch you'll do the same.

As I read this book, I couldn't help but compare it with fictional classics like *Oliver Twist, Huckleberry Finn,* and *Little Women* in the way it evokes both the brightness and shadows of childhood. It is beautifully written, and its flowing narrative just won't let you go.

The difference is that *this story is true,* and it continues to unfold and grow more glorious and thrilling day by day. This is because Ike and Carolyn and the dedicated houseparents in the eight Bethel cottages continue to take in these hurting children and hold and comfort them in an environment of Christian love. They give them positive role models for the first time, educate and redirect their lives, and miraculously give them hope for a future that would otherwise have been unimaginably horrible.

Child of Pain, Children of Joy is a story of miracles, of rescue and transformation, and it is still being lived today in Chattanooga at Bethel. Many people laid the foundation and watered the seeds and therefore are to be honored and praised, but this book focuses on the story of one little boy from Scotland who was dealt a seemingly unfair hand in his early life, but who has become a living demonstration of Romans 8:28 NAS: "And we know that God causes all things to work together for good to those who love God, to those who are called according to *His* purpose."

As you'll see from this book, Ike and Carolyn Keay were clearly called by God to Bethel—which literally means in Hebrew, "God's House"—and this is one heart-filling, thrilling account of God's working through these two dear people to bless countless others. Enjoy it, and then I'll bet you'll want to be involved with Bethel, too.

Who knows, you may even get "hooked," just like I did!

PAT BOONE

Coauthor's Foreword

Several years ago, I wrote a piece for *The Guideposts Christmas Book* titled, "A Bonnie Brae Christmas." It was a memory of my first Christmas at Bonnie Brae Farm, a home where I had spent five years as a boy. It was picked up by a newspaper syndicate and widely distributed to papers around the country.

One morning at our *Guideposts* offices in midtown Manhattan, I got a call from an old friend whom I hadn't seen in many, many years: Ike Keay, the Bonnie Brae boy who had been my childhood hero and protector. He had seen the story in the Chattanooga papers. We picked up on a friendship that had been interrupted more than three decades earlier.

When I learned that Ike had his own children's home, a place called Bethel Bible Village, the wheels began to turn. I suggested he might want to write a story for *Guideposts* about his experiences. That story, which read like something out of Charles Dickens, was published in *Guideposts* in May 1984 under the title "Children of Pain." As a result of this moving account of Ike's years at Bonnie Brae and his work at Bethel Bible Village, Bethel received a spate of donations.

The next logical step seemed to be a book. . . .

Ike Keay is a Christian. I mean a *real*, "if a man strikes you on the left cheek, turn to him the right also" kind of Christian. Collaborating with him on this book was an experience—and not always an easy one. There are very few shades of gray for Ike. Take dramatic license, a useful (and heretofore legitimate) writing technique. It was out. To Ike Keay, dramatic license is suspiciously akin to plain old prevarication. He insisted that while his book might not be polished literature, it *would* be the unvarnished truth. The man's integrity is unassailable.

Collaborating with Ike on his story was a spiritual adventure. He often brought me up short with his transparent, childlike faith. He caused me to rethink my own faith, my so-called commitment to God.

The faith expressed in these pages is no put-on. It is the real thing—simple, direct, and strong. It is a faith that startles and convicts everyone who encounters this remarkable Christian who as a young man of twenty took seriously Christ's command: ". . . Whosoever shall not receive the kingdom of God as a little child shall in no wise enter therein" (Luke 18:17 KJV).

In commissioning this book, the publisher thought it ideal that I had been at Bonnie Brae with Ike Keay. I had been an eyewitness to his life there, and having experienced many of the same traumas, I could help him accurately recreate those years.

What neither the publisher nor I reckoned on, however, was the absolute trauma we would experience in delving back into the Bonnie Brae years. It was excruciating. Knowing that the ". . . fervent prayer of a righteous man availeth much" (James 5:16 KJV), I was frequently asking Ike to intercede with heaven for our project—certain that he, if anyone, has clout Up There.

As the pressure to finish mounted, I began to get an uncanny sense of Someone peering over my shoulder, nudging me to delete this or add that; even guiding me to a disorganized stack of interview transcripts, where I would suddenly spot just the right anecdote for the chapter on which I was working. The Lord was our Managing Editor, no doubt about it.

Not surprisingly, under the bone weariness and above the pressures of time and deadline was the almost palpable sense of God's Spirit, undergirding, overarching, carrying us forward with a strength beyond ourselves. Could we only have imagined Christ miraculously multiplying our time and energy, like the loaves and fishes? I think not. . . .

The other thing that carried us forward through every discouragement was the knowledge that this book might help the children of Bethel Bible Village—children who have suffered, just as Ike and I suffered so many years ago. If this book could somehow help *them,* or maybe expand Bethel's outreach, then somehow we would be helping ourselves . . . the children we were.

For Ike Keay's story is the story of every kid who ever lost his parents and had to go to a group home; every kid who was ever beaten and abused, unloved, or hungry, or scared.

Someone asked me, "Well, when are you going to write *your* book about Bonnie Brae?"

"Oh, I won't have to," I replied. "It's all in Ike's book."

When I repeated this to Ike's brother, Al Keay, one day toward the end of this project, he said, "Yes . . . sure. I feel the same way. It's my brother's book, but it's *my* book, too. It belongs to me, to you . . . to *every* Bonnie Brae boy."

And it belongs to every Bethel boy and girl, too, because in a mysterious but very real way, Ike Keay *is* all of us.

WILLIAM DEERFIELD
New York City
January 1989

Acknowledgments

The authors wish to thank the staff and children of Bethel Bible Village for their support and cooperation during the research and writing of this book, and especially Nancy Speicher for all her hard work. We would particularly like to thank Mr. Ted DeMoss, Mr. Scotty Probosco, and Mrs. Eleonore H. Williams and the board of directors of Bethel Bible Village for their faith in this project and their continuing encouragement.

We would like to thank Alex Keay for his time and input into his brother's book, and the entire Keay "clan": Carolyn, Kimberly, Deborah, Brian, and Alan.

We extend special thanks to Gary Sledge of *The Reader's Digest,* who first saw the possibilities of Ike Keay's story.

We wish to extend our appreciation to the current administration of Bonnie Brae Farm, particularly Anne K. Wardrop, director of development, for allowing us access to Bonnie Brae and for supplying us with background material.

Finally, coauthor William Deerfield wishes to thank Mr. Kenneth Meeks of *Guideposts* magazine for his assistance in correcting the manuscript, and Mr. Van Varner, editor of *Guideposts,* without whose kind cooperation and moral support this project could not have been brought to completion.

Prologue

Bitter Creek, 1962

The day was gloriously, deceptively beautiful. The summer sun hung in a sky of piercing blue. The green trees, the mountains, the lake lay quietly under the warmth of golden beams that poured down upon them like a joyful benediction.

The putt-putt-putt of the boat's motor was the only sound as we headed for the middle of the lake. The sound seemed small, half swallowed by the vast summer silence. The steep forested mountains that rose on either side were reflected in the dark, emerald green water of Willow Lake in North Carolina.

I reclined in the stern of the small rented boat, idly trailing my hand in the water while my wife, Carolyn, navigated. My little girl Debbie, who was not quite two, was sitting on my lap enjoying our family adventure in boating. Her sister, Kimberly, a year older, sat sedately near Sue and Clara, two staff women from the Mountain Haven Children's Home where Carolyn and I were home missionaries.

It was great to lie there in the stern, doing nothing but trailing my hand in the water, soaking up the warm sun and enjoying the day with my wife and children. We had been going almost nonstop for weeks at the home, with the usual thousand and one problems of child-care work, problems that seemed never-ending. We were tired. So it was good to get away for the day.

Carolyn turned the motor off and the silence was total. She grabbed the oars and rowed us toward the center of the lake, the oars making a pleasant splashing sound.

Little Debbie leaned over and, by stretching her tiny arms, managed to put her little hand into the water—just like Daddy. I felt a surge of pride and love.

I myself had been the product of a broken home and the child-care system. For nine years my brother and I had lived in a boys' home in New Jersey, rarely seeing my mother. (Our father was dead.) We grew up in a typical institutional atmosphere, with too many children and not enough adults to give the warmth and love and nurturing children need so desperately. Small wonder that when Carolyn and I married, I vowed my children would receive all the love and physical affection that had been denied me.

But it went beyond my own children. The kids at the Mountain Haven Children's Home, many of whom had been neglected and abused, had fierce needs for parental love, discipline, and caring. Carolyn and I were there seeking to meet the bottomless, inexhaustible needs of those kids, who were aching for love they had been denied—even as I had been denied.

This was my calling, my life's work. Right now I was only a schoolteacher at a home, but my dream was to one day have my own children's home where, with God's help, I could begin to introduce changes that would *really* help mend young, hurting lives. There was so much I could do to improve things for those little ones. I knew I could—and would—if I ever got the chance. The needs were so great . . . so great. . . .

"Ike, honey," Carolyn said, interrupting my reverie, "watch Debbie or she'll fall in! Please be careful."

"Carolyn's right," Sue chimed in. "You'd better hold on to her."

"Oh, she's not going to fall in," I replied, smiling at their concern, "and if she does, I'll just reach in and grab her. No problem."

Debbie was a pretty little blue-eyed blonde who, in contrast to her beautiful, auburn-haired older sister, Kimberly, loved to be hugged and cuddled. Even at eighteen months, she was bright, talkative and curious, and a bit of a dreamer. "Very advanced for her age," was Carolyn's proud assessment. Despite her affectionate nature, she had a bit of the daredevil in her—which was why she was leaning out of the boat at the moment.

I hadn't thought to ask if there were life vests when we rented the boat, but then I was an excellent swimmer, with years of experience as a lifeguard, not only at Bonnie Brae Farm (the home where I was raised) but at Boy Scout camps as well. I had total confidence in water.

When I didn't sit Debbie upright, Carolyn said, "Honey . . . her little body is so short . . . she's going to fall in! Don't let her do that! Please. . . ."

"Okay, Debbie, let's make Mommy happy!" I sat her up straight, cuddling her. She promptly wriggled free and scooted over to Kimberly.

"Well . . . I'm going in for a dip!" Clara cried, removing her terry cloth robe and slipping over the side into the water. She splashed around.

"Oh . . . come in, you all!" she sputtered. "It's great!"

"Guess I'll try it," I said, standing up.

"Sue, will you watch the girls while I row?" Carolyn asked.

"Sure thing," Sue replied. "Come on over here, girls."

I dove off the side of the boat.

"There goes Daddy!" Carolyn cried. Debbie and Kimberly squealed with delight as I struck out for the middle of the lake.

The water was cold but invigorating. I had never seen such dark green water in my life. It was microscopic algae, proliferating in the warm summer sun by the billions. Yet the water seemed clean enough.

About twenty yards from the boat, I rolled over and did a gentle backstroke. All my muscles responded in the familiar watery environment. It felt so good, stretching my arms back and out, feeling the cool pleasurable pressure of the water against them as I stroked easily along, my ears just under the surface, the bright blue bowl of the sky above me.

Then I heard it . . . *screaming* . . . screaming muffled by the water.

Quickly I raised my head and looked. Carolyn was standing frozen in the boat, a look of horror on her pretty face. "Ike! . . . Ike! . . . Debbie's fallen in the water! Hurry! Get her please!"

Sue and Kimberly were peering over the side of the boat at a spot where Carolyn pointed. Kimberly was whimpering.

Righting myself in the water, I swam with quick, strong strokes toward the boat. I wasn't unduly concerned. I'd just grab Debbie and haul her back in the boat. But I was scolding myself for having let her stick her hand in the water. And *why* hadn't I asked about life jackets, just as a precautionary measure? Stupid!

Carolyn was staring with wide, fixed eyes and pointing to the spot where Debbie had fallen in. She was rooted to the spot.

Immediately I was puzzled and disturbed: A person, even a small child, causes ripples on the surface; those telltale ripples are the first thing to look for. *There were none.*

Every second was precious. Taking a deep breath, I surface dove. That was when I got another jolt: The water was so dark green, I couldn't even see my hand in front of me.

Instinctively, I began swimming underwater in a tight circle, reaching out frantically in that murk, where I felt . . . nothing. I continued to grope as I swam in ever-widening circles. Still nothing. *Where was she?*

In my imagination I saw our little girl at the bottom of the lake, tangled in seaweed, struggling. And I saw myself trying to rescue her and becoming entangled, too . . . and both of us dying down there, in the cold weeds and slime. I pushed the horrible image from my mind.

My lungs were bursting. I pushed to the surface, gulping air, then surface dove again, stroking blindly once more in circles.

A minute had already passed, and I hadn't found our precious little girl—*couldn't* find her. Why hadn't I been more careful? Why hadn't I listened to the women when they warned me about letting her lean over the side?

The story of Job flashed through my mind. He had lost his children, too. His words echoed in my brain: ". . . The Lord gave and the Lord has taken away. Blessed be the name of the Lord" (Job 1:21 NAS).

And I remembered what my mother-in-law said when I married Carolyn: "Hold everything with an open hand; never clutch on to anything." I knew that as a Christian, I was only a steward of everything God had given me. My wife, my children—everything that is most dear in life was just on loan to me. He could take them back at any time. *Was this that time?*

"Oh, God," I prayed, as I continued to blindly search the water, my lungs aching, my heart breaking, "if You want our little girl with You in heaven, then You take her, because I know I'm going to see her again, be with her again, for all eternity. So if you have to, God, just take her. But Lord . . . I really do want her back. . . ."

I thought of Carolyn, what she must be going through—the anguish and fear that only a mother can know when her child is threatened. I could see her standing helplessly with the others, waiting, praying as she had never prayed before, to our loving Heavenly Father.

A third time I came up for air. It was almost two minutes. *I knew she had drowned by now.* I'd have to give her artificial respiration when I found her. *Oh, dear God . . . please help me find her.*

It's hard to explain what happened next. Words—a command—cut across my confused, agonized thoughts: *Swim to the boat and dive off so you can go deeper.*

That was crazy! It defied logic. Everything I had learned as a lifeguard told me it was wrong. In saving lives, every split second counts, and I would be losing precious time to swim back to the boat, climb into it, and then dive back in again. And yet. . . .

I would never consider such a move in this life-and-death situation . . . where had the thought come from?

It was God . . . speaking to me.

I immediately swam back to the boat and climbed in. Carolyn still had her eyes glued to the water, pointing with her finger. I took a quick, deep breath and dove off the side.

Now I was much deeper, about ten to fifteen feet down. Once more I began swimming and groping in what was now a dark, hostile environment. Water, the wondrous, sparkling element that had always been my friend, was now my enemy, seeking to snatch my precious daughter from me. I'd die before I let that happen. God—the God in whom I had always trusted—was on my side. He would help me. *But time was running out.*

As I continued to grope blindly, my right hand brushed

something. I grabbed it. *Seaweed.* I was about to let it go when I thought, *No . . . I'd better see what this is.*

With my hand holding onto it, I inched my fingers down and felt a small, hard ball—*Debbie's head!*

I quickly pushed to the surface, aware that there was no movement at all. *Our precious little girl had drowned.* I'd give her artificial respiration. Maybe there was still a slim chance. "Please, dear God," I prayed, "please. . . ."

Just as my free hand was breaking the surface, the light filtering through the first few inches of water glinted in her blue eyes. *They were wide open!* I couldn't understand it. Then I saw her mouth. I expected to see it open, too—she would have swallowed water. But her mouth was shut tight.

I burst to the top and started treading water. She immediately began crying. I was astonished; what a *beautiful* sound! I swam to the boat and handed Debbie to Carolyn. She hadn't drowned. *She wasn't even unconscious!*

I climbed back into the boat and hugged Carolyn and Debbie. We clung together, shaking and crying. "Thank You, God . . . oh, thank You!" I said over and over.

We examined Debbie. She was pale, as if she were going into shock. Carolyn snuggled her to warm her, and we quickly headed toward shore.

By the time we climbed out of the boat, Debbie had stopped crying and her color was coming back. Fifteen minutes later, she wanted to play.

Soberly we talked about what had happened. My foolishness and overconfidence had almost cost us our precious daughter—the very child I had vowed to protect and nurture. I had failed my daughter. I had nearly lost her.

Suddenly it struck me: This near tragedy had been caused by a child's following a parent's poor example. *Leaning over to touch the water like her daddy.* My bad example had almost taken her life. What a lesson!

And what of the other children in my charge, the kids I was sworn to care for at the children's home? How was I failing them?

All at once my foolishness, my human limitations, rose up in my mind's eye. I remembered the words of Jesus: ". . . Without me ye can do nothing" (John 15:5 KJV). They were true.

"Lord, forgive me . . . forgive me. . ." I prayed in my heart. I knew He would. I felt chastened, subdued.

Then another thought occurred to me: *How was it that a child of less than two could hold her breath for more than two minutes?* With all my experience as a lifeguard, I wasn't able to do it.

We talked about it in hushed tones.

"It was a miracle," Carolyn said quietly. "God shut her mouth and kept her from drowning."

I thought of Daniel in the lions' den and how God stopped the mouths of the beasts and saved Daniel's life. In a similar fashion, God had shut Debbie's mouth and spared her life.

In spite of my carelessness, God had been merciful. He had given us back our daughter. And oh, how grateful we were! We returned home, praising Him for His never-failing goodness.

For weeks after, every time I saw Kimberly and Debbie playing together or heard them singing "Jesus Loves Me," I would break down and cry. I thought of the Prodigal's father, who said, "For this my son was dead, and is alive again; he was lost, and is found" (Luke 15:24 KJV). This was our daughter who was dead and was alive again. She was lost and was found, and we rejoiced again and again. I knew then that the words of Jesus were true: "What is impossible with men is possible with God" (Luke 18:27 NIV).

I wish I could say, at the beginning of my story, that we all lived happily ever after, but I can't. The near tragedy on the lake that beautiful summer day was just the beginning of more difficult things to come.

A few months after this incident, God would use us to uncover terrible sin at the children's home, an unspeakable crime that has become a national plague: the sexual abuse of innocent children.

As a result of the exposure, an ugly scandal erupted. There were charges and countercharges. My life and those of my family were threatened, for "not minding our own business."

Again and again God was faithful and delivered us from danger. I'll explain how later in my story.

Suffice it to say that in the face of everything, we remembered that day on the lake when the Lord—or His angel—shut our little Debbie's mouth and gave us a miracle. Later, while we were suffering in that crucible of hate and threats, I'd remind Carolyn, "If the Lord gave us back our Debbie, is He going to abandon us now? Of course not!" And Carolyn would be encouraged.

I had long ago learned to trust Him for a nickel or a dime . . . or a miracle . . . whenever my back was to the wall. And He had always come through for me.

But from a purely human perspective, leaving that children's home devastated us. I appealed to our board of directors four times, asking them to reconsider, to let us stay with those hurting kids, who needed us now more than ever. The board insisted, however, that they could not guarantee our safety. They didn't want our blood on their hands. We must leave.

I remember the day we bumped down the rutted driveway leading out of the home, all our worldly goods in a U-Haul behind our old car. My heart was so broken I could hardly see the road in front of me.

But the Lord would have a new work for us to do. Someplace . . . somewhere.

So we, like Abraham of old, went out, not knowing whither we were going. But in *His* hands. . . .

Part One

"All Things Work Together. . . ."

> And we know that all things work together for good to them that love God, to them who are the called according to his purpose.
>
> Romans 8:28 KJV

> And we know that in all things God works for the good of those who love him, who have been called according to his purpose.
>
> Romans 8:28 NIV

1. Toward Bethel

Clarksville, Tennessee, April 1964

So Jacob rose early in the morning, and took the stone that he had put under his head and set it up as a pillar, and poured oil on its top. And he called the name of that place Bethel. . . . Then Jacob made a vow, saying, "If God will be with me and will keep me on this journey that I take . . . then the Lord will be my God. And this stone, which I have set up as a pillar, will be God's house. . . .

Genesis 28:18–22 NAS

We were cruising along the highway at fifty miles per hour when suddenly, without warning, there was a loud noise directly under the rear floorboard—a sound that was somewhere between a screech and a scrape and then a pop. It was followed by a bumpity-bump-bump. Our new—well, practically new—1960 Rambler lumbered across the highway like a wounded buffalo.

"Ike!" Carolyn gasped as I wrestled the wheel and guided us to the safety of the shoulder.

"I think it's a flat, honey," I sighed, turning the motor off and getting out.

I checked. "It's not the tires," I said glumly.

"Well, what do you think it is?" Carolyn asked, opening the back door and getting out.

"I'm not sure . . . it may be the rear end or the rear axle," I said, getting up and dusting off my pants. "I really can't tell."

"Oh, no," she said weakly.

I could see a service station down the road. "I'll take a walk there," I said. "It'll only take a few minutes. Will you and the kids be okay?"

"We'll wait in the car," Carolyn said. "Come on, girls."

Working in child care, with a wife and three small children, and trying to finish my schooling with no money, I had long ago accepted a life filled with constant challenges.

I believe that when the Apostle Paul declared, ". . . all things work together for good to them that love God . . ." (Romans 8:28 KJV), he meant *everything*—the bad as well as the good, the car breakdowns as well as the new job opportunities. Sooner or later most things are made clear, and those that aren't I have learned to accept by faith.

Besides, from a purely human perspective, after the nightmare we had gone through and survived in North Carolina, where our very lives were threatened, this was just a small matter.

This trip was for a job interview at Bethel Bible School in Chattanooga, the only children's home in the United States exclusively for prisoners' children. If it were the Lord's will that we get there, everything would work out. I needed the job if I were to stay in school and get my degree. Without it, we couldn't make ends meet.

Strange how things were dovetailing so neatly. Covenant College, where I was studying, was moving from St. Louis to Chattanooga. I had asked Ed Steele, Covenant College's business manager, to ask whether there were any children's homes in the area where I might apply for a job.

Ed suggested I call Scott Probosco, a Chattanooga banker who also served as chairman of the board of Bethel Bible School. There was an opening at Bethel and I might be considered.

Ed also said the opening was for director of the school. I replied that they probably wouldn't consider me for a top spot like that because they would want someone with a master's degree. It would probably be a waste of time, but Ed insisted I give Scott Probosco a call anyway.

So I called. I let Mr. Probosco do most of the talking, and when he finally mentioned the directorship, I said, "But Mr. Probosco, I don't have a degree yet. I have been in child-care work for about six or seven years. . . ."

"Well, Ed Steele told me that was your goal—to have your own children's home. Is that so?"

"Yes, sir, it is," I replied. "That's why I'm in school, but—"

"Ike . . . let me call you Ike and you can call me Scotty; I can't stand formality . . . Ed tells me you were raised in a children's home yourself."

"Yes, sir . . . for nine years I was at a place called the Bonnie Brae Farm for Boys, in New Jersey."

"Well," he continued, "Ed feels you have a real heart and love for homeless children . . . that you can empathize with them because you were one yourself. I think that's real important."

"I really do love kids and want to help them put their lives back together," I said, remembering my own blighted childhood.

"Well . . . I have to tell you, Bethel Bible School isn't fancy by a long shot. It's only ten years old and mostly concrete-block construction. We don't have much money. We struggle just to provide the bare necessities for these kids. All we can give them is an education and custodial care while their parents are in prison. We're looking for a man with a master's degree, but I still would like to talk with you about the job. Could you come for an interview?"

We were headed toward Chattanooga for our interview with Brother Floyd Hipp, the founder of the home, when our car broke down.

Now, walking down that highway, I refused to be discouraged because I had a feeling God wanted us in that ministry. This might be my opportunity to have my own children's home. It would be the fulfillment of all my dreams.

Mother would have been so proud, I thought. *She always wanted me to serve the Lord.*

Forty-five minutes later, our Rambler was up on the rack in the garage while the kids played tag in the weeds outside and Carolyn and I got the grim news I had expected from the proprietor.

"You folks ain't gittin' to Chattanooga tonight in this car . . . you snapped the axle right in half," he said, wiping his hands. "I can't get the parts 'til next week."

Seeing Carolyn's look of distress he said, "There's a motel right next door where you can bed down for the night."

A motel. I had just thirty-five dollars in my wallet. Even if we could afford the room, how would we pay for meals—and more important, the car?

I hated to call Ed Steele again. He had already done so much for us; I didn't want to call him and tell him we were broken down—and broke—about two hundred miles from Chattanooga. What was Ed going to do, drive all the way from Chattanooga and get us?

That's exactly what he proposed, bless his heart.

Ed arrived at about midnight. We transferred everything to his station wagon and then woke the kids up. He paid the motel bill and we were on our way.

We got to Chattanooga about 3:30 A.M., the wagon crawling up Lookout Mountain, higher and higher. Ed lodged us in the dilapidated, vacant hotel that Covenant College had recently purchased to build a new campus.

"I can tell you, we got this place for a song," Ed confided with a hint of pride. "They called it Castle in the Clouds."

Looking at the fog swirling outside the car, then turning to rouse the sleeping children, Carolyn remarked dryly, "Hmmmm . . . perfect name."

"Well, I'll be back about nine to pick you up and take you to Brother Hipp's. He lives right in town. He'll probably take you up to see the school. Try to get some sleep, now."

Morning brought a glorious day. The warm, golden sun streaming through the broken windows dispelled the cold and chased away the phantoms of the night. The Castle in the Clouds was no longer sinister. But big! There must have been two hundred rooms of all sizes.

We munched on cereal with no milk and then tried to make ourselves as presentable as we could before Ed arrived. I shaved with cold water. In spite of our efforts, we still felt dirty and wrinkled.

Ed tooted for us exactly at nine, and we bundled into his car for the drive back down the mountain to Brother Hipp's house.

* * *

The Reverend Floyd Hipp lived in a modest house north of Chattanooga. It was so clean and neat, Carolyn was concerned the children would mess things up.

Ed introduced us and Reverend Hipp showed us in to the charmingly furnished, spotless living room. Mrs. Hipp, a kindly, gray-haired woman, brought out cookies, milk, and tea while we talked.

Reverend Hipp was of average height, with gray hair and dark eyebrows. Behind his glasses his eyes were intelligent and penetrating but not without kindness. His whole manner, as he spoke, was one of energetic intensity.

Floyd Hipp had been a prison evangelist for twenty-one years. He had started the school just ten years earlier when six little boys, all brothers, were committed to his care by a county judge. Their father was in prison and their mother was in a mental institution. Somehow they had fallen through the cracks in the child-care system.

"Anyway, those children had been tearing up the little shack they were living in," Brother Hipp said. "They were like wild animals living out there, uncared for and unattended by anybody. They were put out of the place by the landlord, just like they were stray pups or something.

"I remember the day I went looking for them after visiting their dad in prison. He had asked me to please find them. It was a hot day in July when I finally found them; they had been living under a big old oak tree with all their meager belongings in a few cardboard boxes. They were so hungry and scared . . . it was pitiful. In fact, some of them were eating roots out of the ground, just to have something to eat.

"Well, sir, we gave these poor children the first hot meal they had in months. They were our first children at Bethel.

"At first, when I went to folks—businessmen and such—with my idea for a home for the children of prisoners, I got a real cold reception. I was told the kids would already be hardened and ruined and that it would be too late to do them any good. But we kept on going.

"We started out with some property on Signal Mountain, in a

house that had been used as a Sunday school for the children of coal miners. We began in a very primitive way, to be sure. I had only twenty-five dollars in my pocket—but Bethel Bible School was born. Little is much, when God is in it.

"Then in 1956, just after we began to build our chapel and school, the old building burned down at four o'clock one morning. But what seemed to be a tragedy turned out to be a blessing: We were just about flooded with clothes, food, furniture—even lumber and volunteers to help us rebuild.

"Because of the fire, people heard about Bethel who didn't know of our work before, thanks to the news media and especially *The Chattanooga News–Free Press*. And those who knew about us previously were moved by the Lord to give more. Even those businessmen who had said it would never work pitched in. And God raised up some of them to be on our board of directors.

"Now, I can only attribute *that* to the Lord," Brother Hipp said with a smile. "You know, Mr. and Mrs. Keay, I've often thought that men like them would never follow an uneducated preacher like me. People just don't do that. But God laid it on their hearts to help these needy boys and girls. And it has continued through the years."

Now they had fifty-four children at Bethel and had plans to build a new dormitory for sixty more children. All of the kids were children of prisoners—either the mother or father (or both) were incarcerated. Bethel Bible School, he reminded me, was the only children's home in the United States for prisoners' children.

Bethel Bible School, however, was only one of Brother Hipp's ministries. His main calling was to prison inmates. He had a thriving prison ministry, spread across several Southern states. He would drive around to prisons in his station wagon, often eating and sleeping out of the back of it, when he wasn't holding services for inmates or trying to enroll them in Bible correspondence courses.

So Bethel, with its ministry to the children of prisoners, was a natural outgrowth of Brother Hipp's ministry to incarcerated parents.

"Over the years, I saw more and more young boys coming into the prisons—teenagers and even below teenagers, kids eleven and twelve. They came from broken homes where their parents preceded them in sin and crime. Some of these kids' mothers and daddies *taught* them to steal . . . and whipped them if they got caught!

"Why, in one jail cell I found a man with his small boys. They were all in there for stealing; he had taught them. In another jail I came across a woman with her three small children in one cell. . . ."

Listening to Brother Hipp, it was abundantly clear that if the cycle of sin, poverty, and drunkenness could be broken early enough, perhaps these children could be saved from the tragic fate of their parents.

Having given us this capsule history of Bethel Bible School, Brother Hipp inquired about my background. I told him about my youth at Bonnie Brae Farm, my years in child-care work, and my dream of having my own children's home someday.

"Mr. Keay," he said, "I need a man who can carry on my dreams for Bethel, and I like the way you talk. You don't have to start your own home. We have one right here for you."

He paused to gauge my reaction. I think I'd have hugged him right then if in his next breath he hadn't punctured my balloon.

"But . . . to be honest with you, we were thinking of an older man, a man who is really settled, and one who has a master's degree. Our previous director . . ." he trailed off, while I wondered, *Have I come all the way down here for nothing?*

"Brother Hipp," I said, "I told Mr. Probosco I was still in school. He seemed to think that would be okay."

He cleared his throat and said, "No . . . no . . . I really had my heart set on a man with a master's degree. But the fact that you were raised in a children's home yourself is something to be considered. . . .

"I'll tell you what," he said, standing. "Let's let that rest awhile. Suppose we go up to Bethel right now?"

Fifteen minutes later, we were driving up Signal Mountain, where Bethel was located. Frankly, I didn't know what to think about the way the day was going. On the one hand he seemed to like me, but my lack of a degree could kill the whole thing.

At fourteen hundred feet we came upon a sudden gap in the mountain. "That's the Grand Canyon of Tennessee," Brother Hipp said with a trace of pride. Far below, the Tennessee River meandered off to the horizon. In the middle of it was beautiful, forested Williams Island. The entire scene was bathed in the languid, blue-green haze of the southern spring.

The car continued to climb. At two thousand feet we reached the top of the mountain, a vast, fifty-mile-long plateau that is part of the Cumberland Range.

We drove through part of the pretty little town of Signal Mountain and past a rolling, manicured golf course. Carolyn nudged me. It looked like quite an exclusive enclave.

Then there was a dip in the road. Had there been a railroad there, we would now have been on what is commonly called "the wrong side of the tracks," because all of a sudden we were driving past a series of very poor looking houses.

The car bumped sharply up and down, over the ruts and boulders that had suddenly materialized.

"Goodness!" Carolyn exclaimed, clutching the baby.

"Oh, this is nothing," Brother Hipp said cheerfully. "You folks should have seen it when we moved out here ten years ago. Then it was all mud. No electricity or telephones, either."

The boulder-strewn road led through miles of thick woods, identified by Brother Hipp as Prentice Cooper State Forest.

Another ten minutes of being jounced about and we came upon a sign:

BETHEL BIBLE SCHOOL

The sign was rusting and full of holes . . . bullet holes.

As we drove on to the campus, it reminded me of a mission outpost in some remote area. In a word, it was very plain. The buildings were all concrete blocks, painted gray.

We turned right and drove past a low building at least two hundred feet long. "This is our main dorm . . . it houses fifty boys and girls," Brother Hipp said proudly. "I'll take you through it after we eat."

We drove past the heating plant, located behind the big dorm, a thirty-foot water tower, clothing and laundry rooms, and a small recreation hall, and pulled up in front of the dining hall, which Brother Hipp pointed out was Bethel's newest building, erected just four years earlier in 1960. Though designed to blend in, it had a much more modern look to it.

The interior was cozy and attractive, with six to eight kids at a table with a staff member. It reminded me of the dining hall at Bonnie Brae Farm in New Jersey, where I had been raised. As at Bonnie Brae, the appearance of strangers and the founder at mealtime caused a hubbub.

Brother Hipp took us around and introduced us. He talked to the children and tousled their heads. The staff members were polite but restrained.

After lunch, Brother Hipp showed us through that huge dormitory with its long, tunnel-like hall and small, bare bedrooms. Each room contained two or three army cots and some were bunked; all had blankets. The overall impression was cleanliness and austerity. Yet, despite the sparseness of the furnishings, just two or three children to a room was an improvement over Bonnie Brae, with its six- and eight-boys-to-a-room dormitories.

As if reading my mind, Brother Hipp said, "It's nothing fancy, but it's good, solid construction and a lot better than the homes our children come from. Would you believe, Brother Keay, that one of our families of children actually lived in a chicken coop and slept on the manure on the floor?"

You could tell he was proud of this big, plain dormitory. And why not? He had helped build it, block by block, with his own hands, lots of sweat and faith, and next to no money.

He left us for a moment but returned with a long, rolled-up cylinder that turned out to be blueprints. We continued past the sitting room, furnished with a big, worn sofa and some straight-backed chairs, and out on to the front porch. "Now, right out here, folks," he said, unrolling the blueprints, "we're going to build a brand-new dormitory. And it will house sixty children."

He paused, beaming, waiting for my reaction.

I wanted to do God's will. I thought He had directed us here. But I had to be honest: "I think smaller cottages would be better. That's the trend today—family-type settings, with fewer children to a couple. They're not building big central dining halls and dorms anymore because kids need more individual attention."

I was aware I might be shooting myself in the foot. After all, I was on a job interview. But I had to let him know where I was coming from. I wasn't about to take a job under false pretenses. And I knew I could never go along with this idea.

At the same time, I didn't mean to be putting Brother Hipp down. He was a remarkable, dedicated Christian and he had tremendous love for these prisoners' children—kids no one else cared for. But I soon realized that for all his plain, unvarnished goodness and his desire to gather homeless kids as a mother hen gathers her chicks, Brother Hipp knew little of the field of child care. His first love was prisoners. That was why he needed someone knowledgeable to help him.

If he were upset by my failure to rubber-stamp his plans for the new dorm, Brother Hipp didn't show it. He simply pointed out that cottages would cost too much. "We just don't have the means, Mr. Keay."

He had a point. From a practical, dollars-and-cents viewpoint, it didn't make sense to build smaller cottages. He felt they had to go for quantity rather than quality. But I could see a change in philosophy was needed. Children have to get individual attention, and with twenty-five and thirty children to a couple, this is impossible.

Then Brother Hipp dropped a bombshell. If we came, he said, we would probably be living in an apartment in the girls' dormitory, where we would share the living room with the girls. In that way we could also act as houseparents.

I was startled. There was no way we could do that. "Brother

Hipp," I said, "with two girls and a baby boy, we can't live in that small apartment and take care of all those girls. I'm sorry. I cannot ask my wife to do this. It wouldn't be good for her health.

"Besides," I continued, "it was our understanding that you were offering me the position of director. Now I know I don't have my degree yet, but. . . ."

I trailed off, realizing the impossibility of what I was saying. How could I hope to run this entire school and finish my education at the same time?

"Well, Brother Keay," he replied, rubbing his chin. "I don't know . . . I had my heart set on a man with a degree."

"I'm really sorry," I said. "I was looking forward to the job as director, but. . . ." Once again, I couldn't finish my sentence.

"Well, we'll have to think about it," he said. "Let's continue to pray on this."

When we arrived back at the "hotel," Carolyn was pretty upset. "What a disaster!" she exclaimed. "Why did the Lord ever bring us here?"

"Sweetheart, listen," I said. "God sent us down here to look into this. If He doesn't want us here, He'll close the door. If He wants us here, He'll open the door."

"Well, I hope and pray He doesn't!" she declared.

We returned to St. Louis and waited for word. A week passed and we heard nothing. "Obviously, they're not going to call, honey," Carolyn said. "Let's face it; you didn't get the job."

I knew she was hoping that the word, if it ever came, would be negative. I had heard her tell her mother that she didn't want to go to Bethel, even if they offered me the job.

A few days later I got a call from Brother Hipp.

After some discussion, we worked out a compromise. The board of directors was willing to waive the previous demand that I have my master's degree. And they offered me an *acting* directorship for a few months, with a promise that if things worked out, I would be named director.

But they still wanted us to live in the girls' dorm.

Even if the housing had been ideal, I was facing a crucial choice: I knew, in spite of all my good intentions, that I couldn't give this new job 100 percent and remain in school, too.

That night I prayed about it. "Lord, what do *You* want me to do? I've been in and out of school three or four times. You know I want to finish my education."

I felt the Lord leading me to lay out the fleece. If they gave me the job as acting director and also the former director's house (not the apartment in the girls' dormitory), I would accept this position as the Lord's will—and I would give up furthering my education.

There was no audible voice in the night, just the quiet prompting of the Holy Spirit and the peace of God—and the God-inspired wisdom of my dear wife.

"Honey," she said the next morning, "I know I've done a lot of griping about Bethel, and living in the dorm won't be fun. But if this is what you want, it's what I want, too."

I was so touched; for once I was speechless.

"Ike," she continued, "look at it this way: You wanted your degree so you could have your own children's home someday. It's what God wants you to do; you've always believed that. Well . . . God's offering you a children's home that's already been started—and that was the goal of your education in the first place.

"Is the degree itself the most important thing here? No . . . fulfilling that dream of having a home is . . . of being able to help poor kids who need someone—the way you and Al did."

Carolyn was right. I dialed Scott Probosco at his office and said, "Scotty . . . we'd like to come." But I also told him we would not be able to be houseparents in the girls' dorm.

"Scotty, we have three kids of our own, and now we'd have twenty-five more. There is no way Carolyn can take it."

"Ike," he said, "we want you and Carolyn. Give me a day or two to work it out."

Scott Probosco went back to the board and got us the house and all our conditions accepted. Like Abraham of old, we would go to Bethel.

* * *

They say the circle is nature's most perfect form, a mystical shape that begins and ends upon and within itself.

I saw my coming to Bethel Bible School as the completed circle of my life. As I said earlier, Bethel was the only home in the United States for the children of prisoners. Ironically, my early childhood was also blighted by crime and violence. I, too, was a child of pain. Now I would be coming full circle: In the name of Christ, I would be ministering to the hurt and damaged children of criminals—the forgotten victims of crime. In a way, I would be ministering to the child I had been.

More important, I would be ministering to Jesus.

> *Inasmuch as you have done it unto the least of these my brethren, you have done it unto me.*
>
> *See* Matthew 25:40 KJV

2. The Keays of Broughty Ferry

Dundee, Scotland, 1937

And Isaac spoke to Abraham his father and said, ". . . Behold, the fire and the wood, but where is the lamb for the burnt offering?" And Abraham said, "God will provide for Himself the lamb for the burnt offering, my son."

Genesis 22:7, 8 NAS

I was five years old and loved my dad—worshiped him. He towered above me, tall and strong, and above all, good.

On Sundays we would walk together down the streets of Broughty Ferry, the suburb of Dundee where we lived, he in his big woolen suit and I in my little suit. And when a lady would walk by, even if she were across the street, Dad would tip his hat and I would quickly tip my "wee" hat. So polite and gentlemanly was he—and I, too, by example.

One of my early memories comes like a scene in an old movie: We had company and I was sitting on his lap, astride his strong legs.

Suddenly I loudly burped, as small boys are liable to do. Dad got up and, excusing himself to his guests, carried me from the room. Putting me on my feet and getting down on one knee he said, without anger, "Now, laddie, we dinna' do that in company. Never! Do ye understand?"

His rugged face, with the strong, prominent nose, was close to mine; I could see the small bumps under the skin on his forehead. I wanted to touch them but didn't dare. He smelled of soap and talc. It was a clean smell. A good smell.

Solemnly I nodded yes. Then he picked me up and took me back inside and resumed his conversation.

He was Izat senior and I was Izat junior. My brother Alisdair, a year and a half younger than I, was named after my dad's father, Grandpa Alex Keay. (*Alisdair* is Gaelic for *Alexander*.) Our mother was Johanna Christina Keay (nee Smith).

Dad's family owned a prosperous dairy farm, which he managed and had made into a big success, so much so that our family was well-to-do.

My mother's father was a stonemason who brought his family from Scotland to America in 1906. My mother's very early childhood was a happy one, with a loving Christian mother but with a father who was constantly on the go. This happiness was cut short when her mother was stricken with tuberculosis. In 1914 she succumbed to the disease. My mother and her sister and brother were placed in foster homes, where they were treated harshly. Later my grandfather married Lizzy Key, who was my father's aunt. She introduced my parents to each other when she took my mother to Scotland for a visit in 1924.

Dad was smitten by Johanna Christina Smith, with her large dark brown eyes. Even her teeth, which protruded slightly and in another girl might have been considered ugly, instead gave Johanna a curious kind of beauty.

Johanna Smith was paradoxical in other ways, too. Although she was physically delicate to the point of fragility, she had a lively, headstrong way about her which no doubt appealed to our father, who himself was lively and fun-loving. But like her mother before her, Johanna was a Christian.

After their initial meeting and her return to the States, Mother and Dad began corresponding. Shortly thereafter, he came to this country, and in June 1926 they were married.

In 1929 Dad's older brother Alec, who had managed the dairy in his absence, died and my father was summoned home to Scotland to take over. My father proved to be an outstanding businessman, and under his management the business grew and prospered.

Mother wasn't as happy in Scotland as she had been in the States. Nevertheless, she assumed her duties as a good wife. I was born in 1931 and my brother Alisdair was born in 1933.

Our early life was happy. Dad was an athlete who loved

soccer and rugby. I can remember him dazzling me by spinning a ball around his head and bouncing it rapidly around his feet. He would take me tramping through the countryside, up in the Highlands, visiting the ruins of old castles. I recall the excitement of the famous Scottish Games in the Highlands. My dad's lusty cheering prompted me to add my own piping little voice to the roar of the crowd.

I spent most of my preschool years over at the farm with my father, watching him milk and feed the cows and even slaughter pigs. It was a good, wholesome life.

Much of my childhood is a blur, but incidents stand out like scenes in an old film, things that were important from a child's perspective.

I remember a girl of about fourteen, named Moirah, who worked for us at the farm. Moirah would come into our house to visit and play with my brother and me. When Mother was out of the room she used to hug us and say, "You know, don't you, that I'm going to marry your father and take you both away. I'm going to be your new mother."

"Oh, no!" I would protest, frightened at the suggestion. "You're not taking us away from our mommy!"

And she would laugh and toss her dark hair and insist it was going to happen.

Then one day in 1937, when I was five or so, I was playing in the backyard, just outside the kitchen door, while Grandmother Keay was preparing lunch.

My father walked across the farmyard, carrying a shotgun. He entered the pigpen. Then . . . a loud explosion. I went to the barn and tried to open the door. My grandma came running. She pulled my hand off the door handle. Then she pushed me aside and told me to go back to the farmhouse.

That night, Mother called my brother and me to her side. Alisdair and I had been listening to the radio, crying—waiting for our father to come home. We sensed something was wrong.

Mother's eyes were red from weeping. Cradling us both in her arms, she said, "Boys . . . I must tell you something very,

very sad. Your father has gone far, far away, and he will never be coming back again. You must be very brave."

Both Alisdair and I cried harder and we wouldn't be comforted. Why had our daddy gone away? we asked. Didn't he love us anymore? Where had he gone? And why was he never coming back? Later, Mother explained to us that our father had been killed in a tragic accident.

Two weeks later we were taken to a big boat, the *Cameronia.* I remember it had huge smokestacks. We waved good-bye to Grandma and Grandpa Keay from high up on the deck of the boat. Grandma was crying.

Then, from above us came a loud booming sound, and the big boat began to slowly move. We were on our way to America. . . .

3. The Sojourners

For to sojourn in the land are we come; for thy servants have no pasture for their flocks . . . now therefore, we pray thee, let thy servants dwell in the land of Goshen.

Genesis 47:4 KJV

Newark in the spring of 1937 was a thriving working-class town, the largest city in New Jersey. At the time of our arrival, the city prided itself on manufacturing a greater variety of products than any other industrial center in the nation.

In 1937, Newark had a population of some four hundred thousand, a melting pot of nationalities to support its many industries: Irish, Italians, Jews, Germans, Poles, as well as blacks—and at least one Scots family, the Smiths of 52 Hinsdale Place.

It was to the Hinsdale Place house we went to live with our maternal grandparents. It was located in a drab, working-class section in North Newark, bounded on the east by the murky waters of the Passaic River and to the north by Forest Hills, the city's poshest enclave.

I wish I could say that in spite of the unlovely neighborhood in which we lived, our new home was a happy one, but I can't.

Granda' Smith, who at sixty-seven had already suffered a stroke, was a working-class man, a retired stonemason, and he had a rough, workingman's disposition: hard, even mean. Auntie Lizzie was just like him. They both ruled with an iron hand.

I'm only speculating, but perhaps our grandparents felt unfairly burdened that their newly widowed daughter and her two lively boys were interrupting their quiet retirement years. It must be remembered, too, that the country was still in the throes of the Great Depression. Three more mouths to feed would have daunted the kindliest parents.

Mother became a working woman. While she worked five and a half days a week—a grueling schedule for a woman with a delicate constitution—her "wee lambs" were left to the less-than-tender care of our grandparents.

The description of the penny-pinching, thrifty Scotsman is a stereotype that is not seriously insulting, but traditional Scottish "thrift" at Granda' Smith's was closer to plain old miserliness. When we went to the bathroom, for instance, I remember Granda' carefully (almost grudgingly) counting out four sheets of toilet paper. And woe to you if you cheated and used *five!* Out would come Granda's razor strap and you'd get it good across the behind.

Originally their house had been a barn, so it was nothing fancy. Our grandparents were forever running around turning lights out, even in rooms where we were sitting, to save a few pennies. I can still see those shadowy rooms, their solitary lamps lit by low-watt bulbs.

Summer mornings we would be sent out to play and were not allowed back into the house. No matter that we got tired, hot, and thirsty; the doors remained closed. We didn't dare go in. I remember that more than once, my little brother and I were so hot and thirsty we drank from puddles in the road.

Saturday mornings we would be packed off to a matinee, which was only ten cents in those days. Matinees occasionally showed horror films. We would be so terrified during movies like *The Spiral Staircase* or *The Mummy* that we would leave before the show ended. But we knew better than to return home early—both times we made that innocent mistake, we were spanked with the razor strap "for wasting good money"—*twenty cents.*

Of course, Mother was fully aware of the cold, joyless atmosphere at 52 Hinsdale Place, but what could she do? Where could she go, a young widow with two small boys? She made the best of things.

Sunday was the happiest time of the week. After enjoying

Sunday school and church, Mother would take Al and me for walks in the cemetery. It was like a beautiful park, with trees and the sound of bees buzzing among the pretty red and yellow flowers. You wouldn't have thought you were in the heart of Newark. It was like a king's pleasure garden. And except for the gardeners and a few people visiting graves, we had it all to ourselves!

We would stroll along the little paths, hand in hand. The sun filtering through the chestnut trees would dapple our faces. Mother would ask us how the week had gone or would tell us some wonderful Bible stories.

All too soon, the sun would begin to cast long shadows, and its light would become golden, making the neatly manicured lawns and trees like a technicolor movie. It would be time to go, and I would feel an aching sadness. Why couldn't we stay there forever—just our wonderful mother, Al, and me? But it couldn't be. We would go back to the cold house on Hinsdale Place.

For Al and me, life on the streets and playgrounds of this new and strange land was as hard and joyless as it was at home. Right away we were branded because of our Scottish accents.

In Scotland, Dad had been teaching me the rudiments of soccer and rugby. But now I was on my own. I knew nothing about American games like football, basketball, and baseball. In football I was forever having the wind knocked out of me. I could never understand basketball. And nobody picked me for their teams in baseball. A simple game of marbles seemed beyond my capacity. Even the girls beat me regularly.

Marbles weren't the only beatings we took. Both Al and I were occasionally jumped and punched around by bigger kids in the schoolyard or on the way home.

Undaunted, I still tried to be friends with kids in the neighborhood. About half a block away from our poor section was a black neighborhood. The black children accepted us, I suppose, because they, too, were outcasts. Anyway, they didn't seem to mind that we talked funny. We would play at their homes by the hour.

Once, Mother looked all over for us and finally found us at the home of one of our new friends. "Why did you boys go off our block?" she asked as she escorted us home.

"Oh, we were playing with our brothers," I replied. Mother smiled and patted my shoulder. Thanks to her loving nature Al and I were color blind.

The Vander Shalies, a family of Dutch extraction, lived two or three houses down the street from us.

John and Willie Vander Shalie had two daughters, Joan and Jean, who were exactly the same age as Alisdair and me. They were our first real friends in America. It didn't matter to Joan and Jean that we talked with a Scottish burr because they were both born totally deaf.

We lived in Newark for four years. As time passed, I began to adapt to American ways. Either the kids got used to my accent or I began to lose it (maybe a little of both).

There was an incident during this time that still haunts me. A retarded man lived on our street. I suppose he was regarded as harmless. At any rate, he was friendly with all the neighborhood children. He seemed particularly fond of me.

One day, when I was out playing by myself, I noticed this man standing in his driveway. When he saw me look, he waved and smiled his big, simple grin. Then he called me over.

Once I was there, he began strolling slowly up the driveway, all the while keeping up a stream of conversation, asking me about school and who was my favorite teacher.

Then he told me he had to "check something" in his garage and asked if I would come with him. Trustingly I followed.

Once inside the dimly lit, junk-cluttered garage, he seemed to change. His voice sounded funny. Instead of checking something, he moved closer to me. Then he reached out and grabbed my arm. I was afraid. I began to feel like I was having a bad, bad dream.

He took my hand and guided it on the front of his pants, which were soiled. The rank smell of dirty clothes and grown-up sweat made me feel faint with revulsion. Frightened, I tried pulling away, but he pressed my small hand against his body. My lower lip was trembling uncontrollably. I began to cry.

He began unbuckling his belt. . . .

I never told Mother or anyone else about that terrible experience. I knew I didn't want to be around that man anymore. Whenever I saw him, I would freeze in my tracks and turn around and hurry home.

The Fourth of July, 1941, was hot in Newark, with that almost tropical humidity common in midsummer along the east coast, south of New England. But to a boy of nine, the heat didn't matter. It was a holiday, and there was a special excitement in the air! Some of the houses on our street had flags of various sizes jutting on sticks or poles from upper windows, and all day you could hear the distant bang of firecrackers from other streets. After dark there would be fireworks, and Mother said we could stay up to watch. Al and I could hardly wait!

By midafternoon Granda's guests—other elderly Scotsmen and their wives—were gathering in the small front yard at 52 Hinsdale Place, chatting with their thickly burred speech and drinking pitchers of Granda's strong home-brewed beer. We kids would pause in our dashing about to gulp tall glasses of dark root beer, also brewed by Granda'. Oh, did that homemade root beer, chilled with chips from the big block of ice in the icebox, taste good when you were hot and sweaty from running around and the blood was thumping in your temples.

Mother helped Auntie serve the guests. From time to time she replenished our glasses, cautioning us in her quiet way to be careful with our dashing about the yard, lest we upset Granda'. Every now and then, she'd sit down to rest and chat a bit with the guests, patting her pale cheeks and throat with a damp handkerchief. Then Auntie would call her and she would rise and excuse herself and go up the steps into the house, leaning on the railing.

Mother hadn't been feeling well lately. Always thin, in recent months she had lost even more weight so that her cheekbones stood out as her face became thinner and thinner.

As darkness approached, Alisdair and I went with Mother up to our bedroom at the top of the house to see the fireworks over Newark.

The scene stands out so clearly in my mind, even all these years later: Al and I were kneeling by the window with Mother, he on one side and I on the other, watching the brilliant flowers of pink, white, and blue light blossoming in the night sky over the city, accompanied by really grand sputtering and booming that was just thrilling for two little boys.

After the fireworks died away, leaving pale puffs of white smoke dissipating in the warm black sky, and Al and I were excitedly chattering about which firework was the biggest and best one, Mother inexplicably hugged us to her and then called us her "wee lambs," as she often did.

"Boys," she said, "listen to me." Al and I stopped our chattering and looked at her. Her dark eyes, which had grown unnaturally large in the past months as her face had grown thinner, reflected the dim light filtering in from the streetlamp. "Boys," she said, her voice sounding strange and thick, "Mother is sorry to have to tell you this, but she is going to have to send you to a children's home. . . ."

What was Mother saying? She couldn't be sending us away from her. She couldn't. . . .

". . . you boys are going to go to a nice place in the country," Mother was now saying very quickly, hardly pausing for breath. "It's a wonderful children's home . . . really, boys, and it will be *grand* fun for you! There'll be lots of boys for you to play with. You'll be able to pick up eggs from the chickens and milk the cows in the morning. You see, it's a farm, like in Scotland! Won't that be fun?" she said, squeezing me around the waist and suddenly looking down first at me, then at Al, with a strange, forced smile.

She was trying so hard to make it sound cheerful and nice. But it was horrible—the most horrible, frightening thing I had ever heard.

"No, Mother!" I cried, my mouth twisting down at the

corners. "Please don't send us away! I'll shine shoes! I'll sell newspapers! I'll do anything you want! But please, don't send us away! Please. . . ."

Tears were streaming down my cheeks. My breath came in short, hard sobs. Al was crying, too.

"Now . . . now, my wee lambs! Mommy *has* to go away. Try to understand . . . won't you? You must be brave, so Mommy can be brave, too. . . ." Mother's voice cracked. She looked away, out into the night sky that a few minutes before had been glorious with blossoms of light. Now there was only darkness.

The real fireworks had just begun. We all lay down on her bed together, the three of us crying. How could we be torn away from our loving mother? Why?

Mother really did have to go away. Tuberculosis, the disease that had killed her own mother, her older sister, and had decimated her family in Scotland, had now stricken her. It was almost inevitable, given her family history and the inherited delicacy of her own constitution, one stressed by the shock of her husband's death, the move back to the States, and the relentless grind of four years of work.

Because Mother was going to the hospital and expected to die, as her mother and sister had, she didn't tell us a thing about her illness. Later, after we had settled in at the home, her condition was explained to us.

I don't recall whether or not I really believed that Mother couldn't do anything about it, as she insisted. I only knew she kept telling us she could do nothing to change the situation. Her attitude baffled and frightened me: *We were leaving her. We were to go to that home in the country.* Those were the two terrible certainties, and no amount of crying or begging could change things.

After that, things moved swiftly. The next day, Mother and Auntie were packing our things in cheap cardboard suitcases and boxes. I was filled with a dread deeper than anything I had ever known. I was faint with terror and had a constant feeling I was about to be sick to my stomach.

In one of his books, the great Russian novelist Feodor

Dostoevsky describes the feeling of a man being driven through the streets to his execution. He keeps thinking that there is still time. There are still five more blocks to go . . . there are still three. . . .

This is pretty much the way my mind was working the last few days we were at home with Mother. Although there was that sickening dread, each day I thought, *We still have today and that's hours and hours. And tonight . . . we'll still have tonight. And we'll still go to sleep in our own room in our own beds . . . and tomorrow . . . tomorrow, why that's a long, long time from now. And maybe then Mother will call us to her and say it was just a bad dream. . . .*

Two days passed that way. And Mother did not say it was only a bad dream.

We went to Sunday school and church to see our friends for the last time. After dinner we had our final walk in the beautiful cemetery, only it was no longer beautiful; it was a place of death.

Monday, July 7, 1941, was hot and still. Mother and Auntie were unusually silent as they moved about the kitchen preparing breakfast. When they did talk, even about something innocuous like getting the butter out of the icebox, their voices were low. That feeling of awful dread rose up within me.

I looked across the table at Al. Our eyes locked and I knew by the expression in his that doomsday had arrived. I looked down at my bowl, heartsick.

"Eat your porridge, Izat," Mother coaxed.

"I'm not hungry," I said, not looking at her. The corners of my mouth were pulling down. I tried to stop them from doing that, but I couldn't. I put my elbow on the tablecloth, my spoon jutting into the air at an odd angle, and shrugging my face against my sleeve, wiped my eye.

"None o' that now, laddie!" said Auntie Lizzie.

Mother caressed my head. "Try to eat, dear, for me, won't you now?" I sniffled and put my spoon in the cereal that by now had the consistency of library paste. I looked over at Al. He was staring, his eyes moist with incomprehension and fear.

"It's a beautiful place, boys!" she said with forced gaiety.

"There are beautiful green lawns there, and big shade trees and a swimming pool, and really lovely cottages. I've seen them! There's even a wishing well. And boys, remember how you love to take long rides to the lake in Uncle Norman's car?"

It was a miserable drive. Al and I cried all the way, and nothing Mother or her brother, Uncle Norman, said comforted us—or fooled us.

Uncle Norman's 1937 Packard glided down a narrow blacktop road. Up ahead, on our right, was a high fence with a lawn behind it that stretched for what seemed miles, up to a huge building with a tower in the middle of it. It was not the home.

"That's the veterans' hospital, boys," Mother said, pointing. "It's where the sick and old soldiers go. . . ."

A little farther along, Mother pointed to the left. "There, boys! There it is! See?"

Part Two

Bonnie Brae

I want to wake up in the morning,
  In dear old Bonnie Brae,
Where the sun comes a peeping
  Into where I'm sleeping,
And the songbirds sing, "Hello. . . ."

Bonnie Brae Song

4. The New Boy

And when they saw him afar off, even before he came near unto them, they conspired against him to slay him. And they said one to another, Behold, this dreamer cometh.

Genesis 37:18, 19 KJV

We drove slowly up the long, stately lane. The graceful branches of the trees that bordered both sides dappled shadows on the car, while from under the tires came the crunch of gravel.

There was a circular lawn in front of us, shaded by trees. Under the branches I could see the well Mother had told us about. She had called it a wishing well . . . how ironic.

The car circled the lawn and came to a stop under a stone archway attached to a very imposing building.

We were ushered inside to be registered. I don't recall much because I was so scared, though I do remember tiles on the floor and the smell of wax and lemon oil. Both Al and I were sobbing the whole time.

Then suddenly, Mother and Uncle Norman were walking toward the door.

Al and I began to cry even harder. There were hands on our shoulders, restraining us. It was like a nightmare, all crazy and noisy and mixed up and unreal.

Then our beloved mother, who had been our shelter, our comforter, our security always, was gone.

We were taken, still sobbing, to a big house named Kiwanis Cottage. It was the cottage for the youngest boys, eight through eleven years old. Again the smell of wax and lemon oil assailed our nostrils. The rooms were large, with tiled floors and heavy, dark furniture. We cried all afternoon and evening. When we went to bed, I cried silently under the covers. I lay there in the dark in that harsh place with strange boys all around me. I wanted to be in my own room in our house on Hinsdale Place. I wanted my mother! "Oh, God, why can't I be with my mommy? Why did she leave me?" I sobbed myself to sleep.

The following morning, Al and I were introduced to the shower room. Neither of us had ever undressed in front of other boys, and now we had to shower with four or five of them at once in the big shower room, with its slippery floor and smell of chlorine.

We tried to hide our nakedness by holding our washcloths in front of us, feeling thoroughly miserable. Our small size and generally unprepossessing appearance did not escape notice. I stood under the hissing column of hot water, feeling every eye scrutinizing my nakedness. Snickers and taunts were soon echoing off the tiled walls.

"Hey, look how skinny! This little one looks like a toothpick. If he stood sideways and closed one eye, he'd look like a needle! Ha! Ha! Ha! . . . Hey kid, you look like a gopher! . . . Hey, buckteeth!"

Then they began making horrible, filthy sexual comments about us that we had never heard before. It was bad enough that they were poking fun at me. But it hurt me even more when they picked on my little brother. And I couldn't do anything about it. A bell rang for breakfast.

The dining hall had a vestibule with hooks to hang coats in cold weather. Boys were pushing through double doors at either end and into the dining room proper.

There were about twenty heavy wooden tables, all evenly spaced apart, at which seven boys sat with a staff member. The room buzzed with the noise of eighty different conversations. No one spoke to Al and me except to direct us to a table, where we self-consciously slid into our places.

Suddenly the buzzer rang and everyone seemed to freeze in their tracks. The boys around me were bowing their heads, so I bowed mine.

Then a hundred voices prayed: "For Thy many blessings and this food we thank Thee, O Lord. For Christ's sake. Amen."

The food at Bonnie Brae was good and plentiful by institutional standards. The home had its own resident dietician, who made sure we got balanced meals.

Al and I were to have problems with some of the American food they served, particularly corn. We didn't know corn in Scotland, and it was seldom served at Granda's house. I never liked it and it literally made me sick. But the staff member who headed our table ordered me to eat it anyway. I'd sit there staring at that ear of corn. There was no escape. I'd take a few bites and gag, then I would run for the door and vomit. Sometimes I didn't make it to the door and what a mess! For years I had to eat the corn and it happened every single time.

Sociologists say that every group, whether birds or animals or people, automatically organize into a hierarchy based on strength—the pecking order. And no society has a more brutally defined and maintained pecking order than the society of boys. At Bonnie Brae, Al and I were at the bottom of the pecking order. We were soon to learn the rule of the jungle: Might makes right.

We were the "new guys" and therefore beyond the pale—universally loathed and despised. Since we were so little, we were fair game for all the bullies, which meant practically everyone in the cottage.

Most, if not all, of the boys came from broken homes and had grown up in poverty, often neglected and abused by parents who were ignorant and sometimes alcoholic. Every boy, I was soon to learn, had his own sad story. All of them had been rudely taken from their homes and families—just as Al and I had been taken. By inflicting cruelty, they were lashing back at life, hoping to lessen their own inner loneliness and pain. It made them feel better to be more powerful than someone else. But it was about as effective as scratching poison ivy.

On the second day, our housemother called me into the back sitting room.

"Who said you could come in here with your shoes on?" she demanded. "You'll scuff up the floors!" I looked down at my shoes, my face going red with shame. Somebody had told me about that rule, but I had forgotten. There was so much to remember! So much to get into trouble over!

"Did you see those boys smoking in the locker room?" she asked, squinting at me.

"Yes ma'am, they were smoking," I replied meekly.

One of the boys, who happened to be in the hallway, glared in at me, then quickly ran, sliding across the polished tiles in his stocking feet, and disappeared into the locker room.

Quite innocently I had just broken the most important rule of the locker room code of honor: *Never squeal on your buddy.*

As soon as I entered the locker room, I was pushed around by the boys. Then they began punching me and knocked me to the floor.

My lip was bloody and my body ached all over from the punches, but when I saw my little brother, Al, being hit and heard his cries, I yelled, "You leave my brother alone, you!"

"Oh, yeah? What are you gonna do about it?" one boy sneered. And then he punched me in the face.

In the following weeks and months there were so many beatings. Our arms were always black and blue. And it wasn't only punching and getting our arms twisted. There was a particularly fiendish kind of torture they used. While sitting on my chest a boy would reach back and savagely pinch the insides of my upper thighs, which has to be one of the most tender spots on the body. The pain was terrible and the pinches would leave angry red marks that quickly turned to ugly bruises. The bullies would think nothing of giving me five or six of these "horse bites," as they were called, at a clip.

Because of the emotional and physical trauma, I began wetting my bed. This prompted a whole new round of teasing and humiliation. I was made to stand in an ice-cold shower for five minutes or longer, and rinse my sheets. It was just freezing.

In the milieu of the locker room, any physical drawback was immediately seized upon and played for all it was worth. Because of our big buckteeth, Al and I were humiliated with names like "Woodchuck," "Beaver," and "Groundhog."

One summer afternoon, a group of boys marched me out

beyond the grove of pines that formed a windbreak behind the cottages. On the other side of The Pines, as they were called, there was a big potato field. I was terrified and had good reason to be.

My hands were tied behind my back, and I was forced to kneel in the dirt.

Prodding me with a boot, one of the big guys said, "Now start digging up them potatoes with your teeth, Plow!"

"No . . . I won't!" I sobbed.

"Shut up and eat dirt, you little rat!" somebody snarled. A boot kicked me in the behind, sending me sprawling on to my face in the dirt. "Get busy with them teeth, Plow!"

The clods looked like big boulders at such close range. My tears blurred them.

"Dig! Dig, you little buck-toothed—" A foot pressed into my back. I cried out with pain as small stones under me dug into my bony chest and ribs.

Then one of them pushed my face into the dirt.

I was crying so hard I could barely breathe. But fear overcame my revulsion. Very carefully I took a mouthful of dirt . . . and promptly gagged. Steeling myself, I took another bite of dirt . . . then another, and another. . . .

"That's it! Dig them spuds!"

The humiliation of that incident has never faded.

After that, I hid a hammer in the closet in the bathroom between the shelves. When no one was around, I would take it out and go to the mirror and proceed to tap on my teeth, trying to force them in. How I hated even looking at myself in the mirror! How I hated my big ugly fangs! It's a wonder I didn't knock them out. All I managed to do was chip them a little.

With regard to bullying, Bonnie Brae was no different from any home or school anywhere in any era. Who has not read or seen film versions of *Tom Brown's School Days*, or later, *Lord of the Flies*, with its scenes of boyish brutality. Cruelty among boys has always existed and will always exist, even in the best of schools.

I must say, too, that in the 1940s, Bonnie Brae Farm for Boys was a model home for its time. Bullying was never condoned by the staff, and when discovered it was stopped. But it was a

Catch-22 situation: Because of the code of silence imposed on us, we never dared tell any staff member about it.

In the jungle, conventional morality doesn't work. Survival is all that matters. And, if anything, I was learning what I had to do to survive.

As fall moved into winter, I took to stealing out of our bedroom and sneaking downstairs in the middle of the night.

In the back of the cottage, the concrete floor of the darkened coatroom would be freezing under my bare feet. I'd take down eight or ten coats and go into the locker room.

I knew the heat would be coming up at about four or five o'clock in the morning. I would lie down on the coats next to the radiator and curl up, pulling a few of them over me. I'd turn the silk lining of a coat so it was touching my cheek. And I'd lie there secretly, under the mound of coats, in a warm, safe, comforting darkness.

In my desperate loneliness for Mother, I imagined the warm radiator and the silkiness of the coats touching my skin was her loving touch. The aching in me would subside and I'd drift off to sleep, dreaming about my mother. . . .

On December 7, 1941, the Japanese bombed Pearl Harbor in their infamous sneak attack. War fever quickly reached us at Bonnie Brae. Some of the older boys immediately enlisted in the military. One of the boys, whose last name was Sydam, had a father who had been a major in the army. Before long, some of the boys had formed Sydam's Army. They had uniforms and wooden dummy rifles.

Boys who liked the water better formed a rival "navy" under the leadership of a high school fellow named Bachman. They had rafts they would launch on the duck pond, which was down below the barn.

The two rival military groups, Sydam's Army and Bachman's Navy, had occasional drills and military discipline and staged mock battles to see who was best.

Though Al and I were still "new guys," we wanted to join one of the two groups. But nothing was easy at Bonnie Brae. There was a "little" test we would have to pass first.

We were going to have to fight the Cattlin Brothers.

The Cattlins were a little older than Al and me and had bullied us before this. I was scared to death.

The forced fight was staged in the locker room. Admission was two marbles, payable at the door.

Al remembers the big kids putting a chip on his shoulder and daring the younger Cattlin to knock it off. Al was really scared. But the bigger kids surrounded them, screaming and egging them on. Finally, the younger Cattlin knocked the chip from Al's shoulder, and with the same motion he grabbed my brother around the neck in a hammerlock and squeezed. Al never had a chance. He had to give up from the pressure on his neck.

I can't imagine seeing that and not jumping in to stop it. On the other hand, I think it got me mad at the older brother.

I do remember my fight. I recall being scared stiff as they wrapped and tied the towels that served as boxing gloves around my hands. They came halfway up my scrawny arms.

"Kill 'im, Cattlin!" somebody shouted, as we cautiously circled each other. Everybody was against me. I had no friend in my corner.

Cattlin landed the first blow on my nose. I didn't see it coming. I just felt the tremendous pressure, shock, and pain. I tasted blood.

Then I started swinging like a windmill. The locker room was spinning. I was dimly aware of the sea of blurry faces. I felt rather than saw their malicious grinning . . . and loud voices, jeering.

All at once I was standing over Cattlin, who was flat on his back on the floor. I was panting. Someone was grabbing my arm and holding it up.

I had knocked him down! *I had won!*

There was a deafening roar in my ears. Boys were jumping up and down, laughing and slapping my back, rubbing my shoulders.

I was amazed that I could beat up anyone. Up until that time everybody had been able to "wreck" me, as they put it. Now, at long last, *I* had wrecked somebody.

I didn't know it at the time, but winning this fight was the beginning of a turnaround for me. It gave me a tiny bit of self-confidence. I had won the battle and could now join Sydam's Army.

5. One of the Boys

Hear, my son, your father's instruction,
And do not forsake your mother's teaching;
Indeed, they are a graceful wreath to your head,
and ornaments about your neck.
My son, if sinners entice you,
Do not consent.

Proverbs 1:8–10 NAS

I was at Bonnie Brae only a few weeks when a teenage boy, about seventeen, caught me while I was playing by the apple orchard near the pool. He forced me into one of the old storage sheds. It wasn't just the pushing and shoving that scared me. There was something about his manner that reminded me of the retarded man on Hinsdale Place . . . my mouth went dry.

Once we were inside the stifling coop, he made me kneel on the crusted chicken droppings. He was breathing hard and had a wide, fixed grin. Grabbing himself in a lewd way, he ordered me in a guttural voice to perform a sex act on him.

Emotionally, I survived this second molestation because I had to; there was no other choice. And if there were scars . . . well, they were well hidden, because I never dared tell anyone.

Finally, I couldn't take the bullying and pain anymore and decided to run away. But Al wouldn't go with me.

Secretly I packed my suitcase. Very early one morning, I said good-bye to Al. Both of us were crying. Then I crept out of the cottage and made my way down the lane to the main road, my cardboard suitcase banging against my leg.

It was a beautiful misty morning in early fall. A mantle of diamond dew lay sparkling on the field where earlier they had forced me to dig potatoes with my teeth.

As I approached the end of the lane, I began to be afraid. Where could I go? I could try to hitchhike to Aunt Louise and Uncle Norman's house, but I wasn't quite sure where it was.

A mile down the road I heard a car coming, the sound of its motor weak and distant in the stillness of the country morning. I jumped into the field of grain to hide; it could be one of the staff members! The car was coming closer. I could see a man behind the wheel. . . .

The thought of my little brother, Alisdair, suddenly flashed through my mind. How could I leave him alone at Bonnie Brae? And what about Mother, sick in the hospital? If I ran away, it would just kill her.

Sadly, I turned and made my way back up the lane.

Everyone was on best behavior for Visiting Day. As the cottages filled with guests, the boys would cautiously check out one another's families—whose mother or sister or aunt was pretty and whose wasn't—that is, those boys fortunate enough to get visitors.

Of course, our mother was unable to visit us, but on rare occasions my Aunt Louise and Uncle Norman would come with their children, Norman, Mary, and Rhoda. Their visits were a link to our past. But after the first year, the visits became less and less frequent.

So, on Visiting Day, Al and I took hikes down to the Great Swamp, where we tried to forget what we were missing out on by catching turtles and snakes or gathering blackberries. After a while the hurt became less and less, until finally, we no longer expected any visitors and no longer cared. At least not consciously. . . .

The best defense against feelings is to have no feelings at all. Little by little, day by day, I died inside. Outwardly, my life appeared normal—or as normal as it could have been under the circumstances. I was well behaved; I worked and studied. But inside I felt nothing very deeply.

Ironically, the worst aspect of this inability to feel centered on our beloved mother. Because TB is so contagious, we were not allowed to visit her in person at all until we were sixteen. But I remember being driven to the sanitarium, where we would stand in the driveway, looking up to a window.

Soon, a woman in white, her pale face framed by dark hair, would appear at the window . . . like a ghost . . . and wave to us. Even if the weather were very cold, she would open the window and call to us, and we would talk back and forth.

Other than letters, that was the extent of our communication with our mother, two or three times a year, for many years. Small wonder that as the months and years passed, she was becoming a stranger, or at best, a kindly, distant symbol. My love for her was slowly dying.

As time went by, Al and I were no longer "new boys." There were other, more recent arrivals for the bullies to focus on. More and more we were tolerated and then finally . . . *accepted*.

We were learning American games, particularly marbles—the game at which even the girls in Newark used to beat me. We played marbles after school, weekends, and all summer. We played the circle; we played the hole. Our whole economy was based on marbles.

When we weren't playing marbles, we were collecting baseball cards and Dixie Cup lids with pictures of baseball stars. We'd gamble by pitching them like pennies. The guy who came closest to the wall won the other guys' cards. This eventually led to gambling with our pennies, and ultimately to bigger stakes.

There were other activities I was getting into that were less healthy. I began to smoke. We couldn't get real cigarettes, so we'd collect and strip old cigarette butts, add corn silk, and roll our own. We didn't have matches, either, but we were very inventive: We'd light up by wrapping steel wool in toilet paper and then sticking it into an empty light socket, where it caught on fire.

I wasn't at Bonnie Brae two weeks when I saw big guys stealing pies from the kitchen one night and getting away with it. The lesson I learned was, "It's okay to steal—just don't get caught."

There was a locked closet under the stairs at Kiwanis Cottage, where supplies of candy and treats were kept to be doled out on special occasions. It didn't take long for me to figure out that my downstairs locker was built against the rear wall of the candy closet. I began knocking a hole in the wall of my locker. . . .

Then one day, I received a letter from Mother. In it, she wrote that our father had always been a strong, disciplined, physically immaculate man who believed in sports, health, and clean living. I don't remember her exact words, but they went something like this:

> Izat, your dear father never drank any kind of liquor, tea, or coffee. And he never smoked cigarettes. I pray daily that God will help you to resist temptation, and that you will grow up strong, like your father.

I was stunned by that letter. How could Mother know I was beginning to do these things?

Receiving that letter was a crucial event in my life. After reading it, I was challenged to be like my father. As a boy of twelve I made a vow, in his memory, that I would never do any of those things. I wanted to be like my dad—disciplined and strong. Rejecting bad habits was a way I could honor my dead father and please Mother.

Today the handsome white stucco-and-board dairy barn at Bonnie Brae is closed. The cows are gone, and the hill leading up from the duck pond to the barn is thickly overgrown with trees and bushes. They've been growing for thirty years now. Unless you were there in the thirties and forties, you would never guess it had once been a green, rolling pasture hill.

Summers, we used to call the cows up from the duck pond to the barn at day's end, for the last milking. There was good old Susie, and big Red—she was so temperamental you had to watch out for her or she'd kick you while you were milking her. We'd open the barn and all thirty cows went to their stanchions and their supper of sweet-smelling grain, which we had scooped into their troughs.

I can see it all so clearly . . . I can almost smell the pungent mash, the grain, mingled with the odors of milk and manure. I can almost hear the radio that was always on (they said cows liked radio music). The country music would echo off the whitewashed walls as the herd listened, contentedly chewing their cuds. I usually milked three cows in the morning before school and then again in the afternoon.

Outside, the old bull pen, where we kept Ferdinand and Goo Goo, is collapsed and overgrown. It seems like yesterday they ordered all us kids to stay away—to protect what they mistakenly thought were our innocent eyes—as they mated the bull with a cow in that pen. Shoot, all of us kids would be peeking from our hiding places in the hayloft, under trucks, and behind the bushes, getting a forbidden lesson in the facts of life.

After my brief stints as houseboy, waiter, and gardener, I had been put to work at the barn under Herb Graham, the man we respectfully called the "scientific farmer." Herb Graham was tall and craggy with a moustache—an intelligent, disciplined man of few words. He was so dignified and aloof he scared some of the younger kids. But when he spoke we listened, because we knew he was going to tell us something worthwhile.

In my nine years at Bonnie Brae, Herb Graham taught me how to repair farm tools and make angle irons at the forge, to drive a tractor and lime the fields, and the proper way to slaughter animals for food.

Bonnie Brae, to its credit, taught us to work, to be punctual and disciplined—much more so than the average kid living easily at home with his parents. It was like being in the military, with all the hard but valuable training of that kind of spartan life.

We worked hard in that barn, let me tell you. We fed the cows and milked them, strained and sterilized the milk, cleaned the milking equipment, shoveled manure, hosed down the floors, pitched hay into the lofts, shot silage (winter feed) through funnels into the two big silos, and hauled huge cans of fresh milk to the kitchen and dining hall, where we drank it by the gallon.

And in late summer every available kid would be drafted to spend afternoons in the fields harvesting bales of hay, then stacking them in the loft, where the temperatures would soar over one hundred degrees. The cords on the heavy bales tore at our hands, and hay stubble stabbed and scratched our sweat-drenched faces, arms, and chests, giving us "hay rash."

It wasn't all work, though. We loved playing in the hay—wrestling or swinging from ropes and dropping into it, like Tarzan. And when they began baling it in the mid-1940s, we boys would make little secret rooms and tunnels through the bales.

I guessed I loved the animals the most—feeding and milking the cows, caring for the chickens, ducks, turkeys, and sheep. As I got older and stronger, I was put to work at the pigpen, feeding and tending the sows and their broods of piglets.

Those pigs ate well, let me tell you. In the early days, we'd take an old cart, pulled by oxen or horses, to the back porch of the kitchen, behind the dining hall, to pick up the huge slop drums. All the leftovers had gone into these—bread, potato peelings, vegetables, bones, meat scraps. Then we'd get gallons and gallons of milk and mix it all together.

In winter, after a heavy snow, the horses and even the truck couldn't get down the incline to the pigpen, so we'd transfer the slop onto a bobsled.

On those winter days, it was a disheartening sight to see the entire pigpen buried under snow. (It was on the side of a hill.) We would have to dig through six to eight feet of drifted snow before we started our regular chores of cleaning the pens and feeding. And with the icy wind whipping in from the north, that pigpen was cold!

At any rate, before shoveling, we would build a fire under a big, black kettle and heat the pig slop.

That big, black kettle . . . it was like a witch's pot. We used it for everything: to dip dead chickens, prior to plucking them; to heat the slop—and a few less orthodox things.

For instance, there was the time one of the bigger guys, "Bad Breath" Brodsky, who was in Bachman's Navy, had beaten up one of our Sydam's Army guys. They got him down at the pigpen and pushed his head into the kettle of pig slop. They pulled him up and asked, "Are you going to beat up our men again?" He defiantly sputtered, "Yeah . . ." so they pushed his head back under again. (I remember seeing the bubbles.)

But that kettle was mainly for the pig slop. While the slop was heating, the sows would be standing up on their hind legs, hanging on to the boards and snorting, their glistening snouts wiggling in anticipation.

After the slop was heated, we'd haul the drums up on to the platform and pour the mess over the boards into the troughs.

Slaughtering was a gruesome business. By the time I was sixteen, I was doing a lot of it: chickens, turkeys, sheep, pigs, and even cows.

My exposure to all this—slaughtering animals and hard work in the fields, the cow barn and the pigpen—was having its effects: I was becoming strong, self-reliant, more sure of myself. I was preparing for the real world. And I was growing up . . . fast.

The story of my years at Bonnie Brae would be incomplete without some mention of schooling. Our education (which we got off campus in township schools surrounding the farm), important though it was, was almost peripheral to our life at Bonnie Brae, running parallel to it but separate from it, and overshadowed by our life at the farm.

And whereas children living at home with parents deal with one institution—school—from which they can escape at the end of the day into a (hopefully) relaxed, homey, and loving environment, we Bonnie Brae boys were dealing with two separate institutions. So there was never relief from the demands of one or the other. But when there was a conflict between the two, you can be sure Bonnie Brae's interests and/or rules always took precedence over those of the public schools.

When I first came to Newark from Scotland, I was way ahead of my classmates because the schools in Scotland had been more advanced. School had never been a problem for me. Until Bonnie Brae. . . .

The sad fact is, I had been so traumatized by the agonizing separation from my mother and the brutality of the boys that I couldn't handle school that first year. I flunked fifth grade and had to repeat it the following year in a tutorial setting at Bonnie Brae.

My primary concern, however, wasn't focused on school but on a longing to be really accepted by the guys at the farm. My brother was smart, but being smart didn't do it, not in surroundings where might made right and the rule was brute force. You could have the IQ of a potato but that was okay, as long as you were big and tough. Well, I wasn't that smart, or big, or tough.

There was only one other way to gain acceptance: *sports*. At Bonnie Brae, sports was everything.

I didn't have much to work with. For the first couple of years, I was a scrawny, underweight kid.

My size and weight weren't the only obstacles to my dream of becoming an athlete. Except for marbles, I was a big fat zero at games. I couldn't catch a football or a baseball, and I was a coward in the swimming pool.

However, Bonnie Brae had a great athletic program. We had a big playing field for football and baseball. We had a gymnasium for basketball, boxing, wrestling, and tumbling. We also had an outdoor swimming pool and clay tennis courts. But most important of all, we had an outstanding coach, Stephen Tomczek.

We had our own football, baseball, and basketball teams on campus and we played local prep schools. I was determined that I was going to be part of all that—to make the teams and do my best.

It is said the primary ingredient of success in any field of endeavor is not skill or talent but perseverance. And that's the one thing I had. When I struck out in baseball, the kids jeered.

But Coach Tomczek didn't jeer. He kept putting me back in the lineup. And I kept trying.

Finally, one magic summer afternoon, I swung the bat and connected with the ball. *A miracle!* The next time up I hit it again . . . and the kids stopped jeering.

It was the same in tumbling. I can't remember how many times I hurt my neck or got mat burns trying to do flips, or got the wind knocked out of me from landing flat on my back. But eventually, I became a decent tumbler . . . and then, with more practice, and guidance from Coach Tomczek, I was becoming an accomplished gymnast.

It was the same with swimming and football and basketball. Basketball, in fact, became my favorite sport. When I was in high school, I was so good that I was made captain of our high school basketball team—as well as captain of the baseball and football teams at Bonnie Brae. I had become an all-around athlete.

Paralleling my growing interest and skill in sports was my involvement in the Boy Scouts, which gave me additional skills and self-confidence and a certain flair for leadership.

I was in Scouts for years. I loved it and took it very seriously. Every summer I went to Scout camp; I attended statewide scouting jamborees; I earned merit badges and eventually went on to become an Eagle Scout.

Although I was excited about Boy Scouts, and although our beloved scoutmaster, the Reverend George Rath (later Bishop Rath), was also the rector of the local Episcopal church, I had no real interest in religion. I did own a Bible but I seldom read it.

We were required to attend church every other Sunday. That was because in those days our parish, All Saints Church in Millington, was so small it could only accommodate forty or so of us Bonnie Brae boys. So only half of us could attend on a given Sunday. Even so, we took up a third of the pews.

We must have been a motley crew, arriving in our old blue bus, pushing and jostling one another as we entered the church (a charming little ivy-covered stone building with a squat tower, capped by battlements—a typical English country church).

Of course we all wore suits and ties (though many a tie was

askew and many a shirttail was escaping), and we were supposed to be on our best behavior. But I wonder how the other parishioners felt about having the serene atmosphere of their pretty little church disturbed by a pack of irreverent, whispering, snickering, restless, pinching, punching, poking . . . boys.

As we moved into our teen years, we looked forward to the meetings of the All Saints Young People's Group, which were held at the rectory on Sunday evenings. I know we had a great time at those meetings, but we didn't learn too much about God. Though I was eventually elected president of the Young People's Group, the Lord was not exactly the most important subject on my mind. I was there because of the girls.

I had several girlfriends while I was in high school, but my most serious relationship, with a pretty blonde named Martha Baldwin, was not until the end of my junior year.

Since Martha's house was next to the church, I went to church whenever I could. Though we were required to go to church only every other Sunday, I began going every Sunday in order to spend more time with Martha. I even sang in the choir, because Martha was in it.

School, sports, scouting, church, girls . . . it was a time of exploration, and developing physical and social skills.

My early life at Bonnie Brae had been full of horrible trauma; now, all that seemed unimportant and was nearly forgotten. I was coming into my own at the farm and at Bernards High, too, thanks to the many people who had a part in my life—and thanks most of all to the prayers of my invalid mother to a loving God, who is still, to this day, molding the clay under His watchful eyes.

Yet, O Lord, you are our Father.
We are the clay, you are the potter;
We are all the work of your hand.

Isaiah 64:8 NIV

6. The Pride of Life

Rejoice, O young man, in thy youth; and let thy heart cheer thee in the days of thy youth, and walk in the ways of thine heart, and in the sight of thine eyes. . . .

Ecclesiastes 11:9 KJV

Mother was a real fighter. Although the disease had ravaged her frail body, she didn't die. Stubbornly she hung on to her faith in Christ and to life, looking forward to that day when she would be reunited with her two "lambs," who were growing up without her. She remembered all too well the loss of her own mother to TB, when Mother was only ten. Al and I had already lost our dad; she couldn't bear the thought of leaving us orphans.

In 1945, Mother was so improved she was released from the sanitarium, and a few times she was able to visit Al and me at Bonnie Brae. I was about fourteen at the time, and it was so special when she came out to see us. We walked about our beautiful campus or sat talking beneath the towering oaks. We greatly enjoyed her visits. But tragically, Mother had become something of a stranger to me. When I needed her, she had been taken away from me. Amid all that pain and hurt my ability to feel and love had been greatly diminished. Yet neither she nor I realized what was taking place.

Shortly afterward, Mother's condition suddenly worsened. She was admitted to another facility, the Bergen Pines County Hospital in Paramus. The TB had spread to her other lung. Our hopes of being together again, as a family, were shattered.

When her health permitted, Mother wrote to us twice weekly, letters filled with love and encouragement. "My Dear Boys," a typical letter would begin. "My thoughts are much with you both today. . . ."

About this time, Mother wrote a prayer-poem, which we later found among her papers. In it she expressed her human fears and desire for courage to face those terrible operations.

Here is the first part of that prayer:

My Confession

Oh Christ, my Lord, I turn
to Thee, as through operations
I go.
For courage and strength
and guidance too can only
come through Thee.

I am such a miserable coward,
Lord. Why do You bother
at all,
To hear my cry? Please stand by
when my faith is so weak
and small.

Forty long years have I
lived, Lord, with only a few
for Thee;
What a waste of life with
nothing but strife, for
not looking up to Thee.

Just give me another
chance, Lord, that's all I ask
of Thee,
To work for my Master, oh
so divine, Who thought, so
much of me. . . .

Mother was to live another ten years, which was really a miracle, considering how the disease and five major operations had ravaged her.

In 1947, when I was sixteen, I was finally allowed to go up to Mother's room at Bergen Pines. Some kindly soul bent the rules and allowed my brother, who was not yet old enough, to go up with me.

Mother had just come out of one of those horrendous operations. In a futile attempt to arrest the disease, it seemed the doctors were almost literally cutting her to pieces. By the time of this visit, Mother had had seven ribs and five pieces of rib removed, plus half of both shoulder blades. Half of each lung was gone. Even if she survived the operations, she would be an invalid for the rest of her life.

As we stood by her bed, I tried to hide my feelings of shock. We had never seen her up close like this . . . with the pain. The gaunt face was that of a woman years older than I knew my mother was. The outline of her pitifully frail body under the sheets was like that of a child.

We were really hurt. Only then did Al and I fully realize all the pain and suffering she had endured.

Was this aged, wasted woman with the feverish eyes, who clutched my strong hand with her thin, blue-veined one—was she the beautiful dark-haired mother I had once adored?

We returned to the farm depressed at what we had seen, wanting to do something to ease Mother's pain, but feeling totally helpless. And life at Bonnie Brae and school ground on. . . .

That year the administration at Bonnie Brae sent Al and me to an orthodontist to be fitted for braces. It cost thousands of dollars. Our teeth had to have been pretty bad for the farm to go to that expense.

Before I could have them put on, I had to have eight teeth pulled. Gradually over the next few years, my teeth, and the entire configuration of my lower face, became more and more normal. Having my teeth straightened was one of the most wonderful things that happened to me as a teenager. I never forgot those painful years when I was teased and bullied so much because of my buckteeth. Looking "normal" and fitting in is very important to any child's self-esteem.

Because of my athletic success and friendliness, I was becoming a popular figure at school—an unusual achievement for a poor boy from Bonnie Brae at affluent Bernards High School.

At the end of my junior year I was honored by my fellow students by being elected student council president. I accepted the office with a mixture of humility and happiness. It was a wonderful honor for a boy from a children's home, as well as an honor for Bonnie Brae.

I was now one of the bigger guys. The bullying had long since stopped. I could have been the bully now, had I chosen to go that route. But I never did. I remembered what I had endured those first few years, and I had no stomach for beating up anyone.

One of the other big guys was Anthony Salerno. He was my best buddy. Tony was a bright, handsome Italian kid, but a notorious bully.

One summer, he and his henchmen in Gould Cottage were making life miserable for the littler guys. When I heard about it, I marched over to Gould to confront Tony. I was surrounded by an ecstatic, ragtag group of little guys who had been his victims.

"What's up, Ike?" Tony said, when we walked into the locker room.

"I hear you've been picking on these little guys."

"What's it to you?" he sneered.

"These guys came to me for protection, that's what! And I'm telling you to knock it off!"

Suddenly the lunch bell clanged. We stood there, staring at each other. The little guys crowded behind me, as if for protection.

"It's time for lunch," Salerno said. "I ain't missin' lunch for this. I'll talk to you later." With that, he turned and with elaborate casualness strolled out the back door.

"He's a chicken!" a little guy piped up.

"Yeah . . . he's scared o' you, Ike!" another kid chimed in. "Boy . . . you sure told him good!" They were all milling around, patting my back and feeling my biceps, partly out of satisfaction and admiration and partly for reassurance that my muscles were as big as they looked.

* * *

I was made a house captain. At the time, there was an assistant director at Bonnie Brae whom I'll call Mr. Pembroke. He had not yet been exposed as a child molester, although it was common knowledge among the older boys, who were his chief victims. He hadn't approached me yet, but I knew it was only a matter of time. And Pembroke's room happened to be in Kiwanis Cottage, where I was house captain.

One night, he crept down the hall and tried my doorknob. It was locked.

The next morning he gently admonished me: "Ike, you should leave your door unlocked. It's against fire department regulations to have any locked doors in the cottage."

That was a lie. I wasn't taken in by him in the least. The next night, after I had gone to bed, I heard the doorknob turning. I kept perfectly still. Then he said in a low, insistent voice, "Open this door!"

I stayed in bed, pretending to be asleep. The knob rattled again in the dark. Then he started banging on the door and barked, "Open this door, or else!"

I was scared, but I stayed in bed. Then I heard him moving away.

The next day, Pembroke was frustrated and furious. "Keay, I thought I told you to leave your door unlocked! It's against regulations!" I stared off into space. I could feel him glaring at me.

"Now do as you're told!" he said. "And I don't want to have to speak to you about it again!"

I never did unlock that door, and he never spoke to me about it again. A few months later, the scandal broke and he was fired immediately. Charlie Group, the director, called me into his office and asked, "Ike, did you know what was going on?"

"Yes sir, I did."

"Well, why in the world didn't you tell me?"

"I was afraid to, because I really didn't think you'd believe me."

"In the future," he said, "if *anything* like this happens, you let me know."

* * *

After nine years, my days at Bonnie Brae were finally coming to an end. I had several college scholarship offers, including one from the church. The Reverend Rath had said the diocese would pay my way through college and seminary—and provide for Mother. And our guidance counselor at Bernards High told me there were other scholarships available because I was a student leader and an athlete.

Before going to college I planned to take advantage of an invitation I had received to go on safari in the Belgian Congo (now Zaire), to study and identify exotic birds. For a teenager who loved nature and the outdoors as much as I did, it was a dream come true. The future lay bright and shining before me!

Then it happened. In early April 1950, my senior year at Bernards High, Charlie Group called me into his office one blustery day, when the wind was scouring the dead leaves from the wide lawns of Bonnie Brae.

"Ike," Charlie said, "we've learned your mother will be released from the sanitarium this coming fall or winter. Isn't that good news?"

I was stunned. *Mother . . . coming home?*

"Of course, we know you have plans for college and for that expedition to the Congo," Charlie was saying, "but you know, Ike, you're the older son . . . and your first responsibility is to make a home for your mother. . . ."

What . . .? What is he saying about making a home?

Then I was told that there was an opening in the mail room at Esso Standard Oil (now Exxon) in Elizabeth.

"It's a good opportunity," Charlie said. "It's a fine company—they have excellent benefits. You'll have a good future with them. And they want a Bonnie Brae boy."

"But . . . but school won't be over until June . . . my graduation!" I stammered.

"Ike," he replied, "the job is there *now.* They can't hold it until June. We've already spoken to the high school. They're willing to let you leave early to take this job, because of your mother.

"You can come back for your final exams and graduation."

I stood there a moment, unable to speak. I was disappointed. No . . . *crushed*. Going to work meant giving up my chance of a college education! And these last three months of high school had promised to be a time of winding down and fun. I'd miss out on the class trip, the class picnic . . . all the private parties . . . I was the student council president! I would have been right up there, with all the most popular kids, having fun, being part of things! And now. . . . Well, it just didn't seem fair!

"Ike, we know how hard it will be to postpone college, but maybe you can go . . . later. And that bird safari to Africa, well. . . ."

My college scholarships! My trip to the Congo! My life . . . my future. All of it was gone . . . just like that!

I was so hurt. Sharply conflicting thoughts of filial duty and my own desires roiled within me. Yet, not a sigh escaped me; not a muscle twitched.

I was in perfect control. . . .

Almost as if it were someone else's, I felt my head nodding up and down, and I heard, as if from a long distance off, my own voice murmuring, "Yes . . . yes . . . okay . . . I see . . ." to everything he was saying. I suddenly realized I had to say something, *do* something.

"You know . . . we don't have . . . uh . . . an athletic director," I said to Charlie. "Well . . . uh, why can't I stay on after graduation as athletic director, maybe a relief houseparent? And . . . uh, maybe I could get a place for my mother over in Liberty Corner. . . ." I looked at Charlie.

If he agreed to that, at least I'd be able to enjoy the last two months of school, and maybe even go on that bird expedition. There would be no major disruption in my life and no reason for me to leave early to take some job on the outside. *And I really wanted to stay.* I just loved sports and thought I could make a good coach. . . .

Charlie was giving me a long, sad look.

"Ike," he said in his firm, no-nonsense way, "you can't stay here. You can't hide from life. You've got to get out in the world. After you've been out there for three years and have given it a good try, if you want to come back, come and see me. We'll talk about it. That's the way it has to be."

At that, I lost it . . . me, the guy who never felt anything. Big as I was, I began to cry. I tried to stop it—I was so ashamed—but I couldn't. I lowered my head so they wouldn't see, but my shoulders were shaking from my sobs.

Mrs. Day, the farm's social worker, came over and touched my arm. "There . . . there," she said in her soft voice, as she patted my arm, "it's going to be all right, Ike . . . you'll see. Why, I can remember the day you came here, as a little boy. And now . . . I'm seeing you off, and you're a fine young man! We're so proud of you, and we know Mother is, too. And you're going to have a good life, and you'll be a success, because you're honest and a hard worker. . . ."

"Now, pull yourself together," Charlie said, his voice firm but not unkind. "And get yourself back up to the cottage. You're a man now."

Two months later, just as spring erupted into warm, languid days . . . the last wonderful, bittersweet days of high school . . . I prepared to leave Bonnie Brae.

The last day arrived. I was all packed. Before I left, I took a last walk around the campus. Off in the distance, the hills were tinged with palest spring green. Closer, down the hill and up in the orchard, the apple trees had erupted into a riot of white blossoms. Nostalgia, like a gray stone, pressed upon my heart. I had seen so many springs, and now . . . now I had arrived at the last one. . . .

I strolled past my old cottage—Kiwanis—where I had been bullied. There, on the side foundation, were the initials I had put there when I was twelve: *I.K. loves J.C.* (one of my elementary school girlfriends).

I walked down past the barn, the infirmary, all the way down to the pigpen. When they heard me coming, the sows stood on their hind legs looking over the boards, wanting to be fed. Patting their heads, I gave them some corn one last time. I thought of Little Runt, my pet piglet. . . . he was long gone.

There was the old black kettle, where they almost drowned Bad Breath . . . and the spot where I fell on that rusted pitchfork. . . . So many years, so many memories!

It was time to go. I cut up the back way, past the gardening shed, through the apple orchard. I thought, *This is the last time I'll be walking this way as a Bonnie Brae boy, forever and ever. . . .*

Tears were suddenly in the corners of my eyes. I loved Bonnie Brae Farm . . . I loved it! This place that I had hated so much when I arrived, I now loved! I had cried terribly when I came here. Now I was crying again because I was leaving. I was losing my home a second time. It wasn't fair; it hurt so much!

Childhood was over. School days were over. Dreams were over . . . I had awakened to harsh reality. I was about to begin a new job and a new life as an adult and the sole support of my mother.

I remembered a game Al and a friend and I had played years before, when we first came to Bonnie Brae.

As I strode under the apple trees, I could almost see them again . . . *three skinny little boys in baggy shorts, galloping on make-believe horses in the early morning, just as the sun was coming up. Through this very orchard they ran, slapping their thin thighs. On they went, over lawns pearly with dew, up and down the hills, past the barn, the coops, and sheds, lost in a wonderful world of imagination where dreams come true. On and on they galloped . . . and as they went, the morning sun was turning the mists that swirled around them into bright, shimmering gold. . . .*

7. King Richard

Honour thy father and thy mother. . . .

Exodus 20:12 KJV

During the course of the next two years, somehow my name was changed. Mother and Auntie dubbed me King Richard.

They recalled that Richard the Lionhearted had returned to save medieval England in its hour of peril. And I had returned from Bonnie Brae to rescue two helpless women.

As silly and playful as the name was, it was a high compliment coming from my grandmother, as well as a constant reminder of my duty toward those I loved. Like King Richard of old, I vowed it was a duty from which I would not swerve.

I began working at Esso Standard Oil in April 1950. Mother wasn't due to get out of the sanitarium for several months.

At first I stayed with Aunt Louise and Uncle Norman. Each morning I'd drive to my job at Esso, and twice a week I'd go out to see Mother at the hospital.

At Esso, I began working in the large mail room, sorting incoming mail and handling outgoing correspondence.

After a few months, I was promoted to addressograph operator. I addressed thousands of envelopes as well as handling the mail.

What a happy day it was when Mother was finally released from the sanitarium. It must have been like being released from prison. Free at last!

I moved from my temporary home with Aunt Louise and Uncle Norman to Newark. Ironically, Mother and I were once again obliged to live with her father, Granda' Smith, and Auntie, as we had done all those years ago when we first came to America.

The old couple had given up their home on Hinsdale Place

and now had an apartment in a public housing project. It wasn't bad living with Granda' again, because both Granda' and Auntie had mellowed in their old age.

In 1951, my brother Alisdair graduated from Bernards High and joined us at the apartment for the summer. It was the first time we were reunited as a family in ten long years!

Then Granda' Smith had a second stroke—a very severe one. On July 4—the tenth anniversary that Mother had told us the terrible news that we were going to be taken away from her—Granda' finally died, without regaining consciousness.

That summer, we were once again faced with a war. This time it was the Korean War, which President Truman was calling a "police action." Either Al or I would have to enlist. The problem was we both wanted to. In fact, I had dreamed of making the military my career, but with Mother, and now Auntie, to care for. . . .

Besides, if Al went in, he'd have a chance for a college education under the GI Bill. And if one of us deserved college it was him. Also, since I was the older son, the responsibility of our mother's care really was mine.

So, that August Al joined the air force. Already our reunited family had shrunk by two.

Shortly after Granda's death and Al's departure, Mother, Auntie, and I moved to an apartment in Belleville, a nice residential town next to Newark.

We had an attractive basement apartment in a house owned by an older couple. It had two bedrooms, a kitchen, a living room, and bath, and its own outside entrance. It was modest but quite nice.

Of course, Mother was an invalid. She could walk, but only very slowly for short periods, as she always had difficulty breathing. But the new apartment was a big improvement over the projects, where I had to carry her up three flights of stairs after church, two or three times a week, and when she wanted to go shopping.

Mother didn't want to be a burden on me, and she was never that. It was my privilege to care for her. She had carried me as a baby, first in her body and then in her arms; now that I was a strapping young man, it was my turn to carry her. And I did; with great tenderness and care, I would hold her frail body in my arms and carry her whenever necessary. She was as light as a child, her head sometimes resting on my shoulder. . . .

For their part, Mother and Auntie couldn't do enough for me. After all, I was man of the house, the breadwinner, the one on whom they depended. They fed me like a king and did everything to make me comfortable in our modest home.

Because our rent was more expensive, I took a second job one or two nights a week and on Saturdays, working in a gas station. I worked hard, changing oil, pumping gas, cleaning windshields.

One day in 1952, Mother told me about a religious camp where I could meet Gil Dodds, who was then a world champion mile runner. What's more, she said, there were twenty-six different sports in which I could participate—and lots of girls.

Mother, of course, knew my two loves—sports and girls—and she also knew that I needed some time away from the two jobs I had been holding down.

The name of the camp, Mother said, was Word of Life Camp. It was run by Jack Wyrtzen, a well-known youth evangelist. I recalled her listening to him preaching on the radio, though I had never paid much attention.

To tell the truth, I hadn't paid much attention to religion at all. I had certainly been exposed to it from earliest childhood. Yet I never really understood it or appropriated it in a deep way. It had not become a part of my life.

As a teenager, I knew what the Book of Common Prayer said, and even some of what the Bible said, but it left me unaffected—as if God were a divine moth, beating His wings futilely against the windows of my understanding. I really didn't understand any of it because I wasn't interested in spiritual things.

And yet I had a churchgoing Mother who loved God. Through the years, Mother tried to turn me toward Jesus Christ. She had been a Christian since she was a young girl. But after she was struck down by TB and not expected to live, she became even more committed. Her letters to us during our Bonnie Brae years were full of her prayers for us and all kinds of biblical references.

I still have one letter she sent to us with a Bible. It is dated January 1947:

> My Dear Izat & Alisdair:
>
> This is the Book divine, "The Living Word," which God gave to man. Cherish it, hallow it; and I pray, trusting it will always take first place in your daily living.
>
> You will find many markings put in these precious pages by me, not only for my own benefit but for yours, Izat, & yours, Alisdair.
>
> Christ Jesus died that we may have life and have it more abundantly. . . . We must choose between the world and Christ; we cannot serve two masters—the way of the world is exciting [but] it cannot provide peace & joy that comes when we consecrate our lives to the Master and His way of the Cross.

I loved her letters. But Mother's deep pleadings for us to turn to the Lord simply went over our heads, and I really wasn't interested. Though I suspect it was making a subtle impression, laying a foundation on which others would later build, at the time it was only words on paper.

After we began living together, I could ignore Mother's intense faith less and less. Many mornings, very early, as I went past her room getting ready for work, I would see her on her knees by her bed, her Bible clasped to her breast, head bowed, lips moving in a silent prayer. Perspiration beaded her brow from the sheer physical effort. She gasped for breath . . . the breath her mutilated lungs could never get enough of. This was my Christian mother. Yet though I respected and even reverenced her faith, it left me untouched.

Then came 1952 and her suggestion that I attend the Word of Life Camp, with twenty-six sports and even more girls.

Though Mother had ulterior motives in getting me to go, I had simple motives, and they weren't all wholesome. So I went, in the prime of youth—I was almost twenty-one—to pursue my two main interests in life.

When I got up there, however, and boarded the boat to get to the island where the camp was, I was shocked to see a crowd of young people eighteen to thirty, all memorizing Bible verses! I couldn't imagine anybody doing that.

Word of Life Camp was on beautiful Schroon Lake, nestled in the Adirondack Mountains of New York State. Beautiful as it was, after seeing all those open Bibles, I was wondering, *What am I doing in this place?*

I arrived on a Saturday and that evening there was a rally. And there was another one on Sunday! These rallies were full of enthusiastic singing by the kids, and preaching by Jack Wyrtzen and Larry McGill.

I really enjoyed the excitement, but spiritually I sat through both services unmoved. I was just looking for a good time. I had no sense of my sinfulness or my need of God.

I had taken my cousin Norman Smith (Uncle Norman's son) to camp with me. He was three or four years my junior. After the service on Sunday one of the counselors, Larry Doyle, said, "Ike, you'd better talk to your cousin. He doesn't seem to be living like a Christian. . . ."

And I heard myself saying to this guy, "I don't think *I'm* a Christian. . . ."

It was strange, because at home I was now attending the same Bible-believing Baptist church with Mother that I had attended as a child in Newark in 1941. And, irony of ironies, I was teaching Sunday school! I was even in charge of the young people's group! *And I wasn't even a Christian.* I had what the Bible refers to as a "form of religion," an imitation. I was, in short, a religious fake.

Not that I was an *intentional* fake. But by this time, I was conditioned to hearing the Gospel and giving the right responses, without ever having it penetrate.

Besides, I was not a deep thinker. Not once in all my years at Bonnie Brae, or after, did I ever seriously ask myself, *Is there a*

God? I passively assumed there was one. I believed in God and in Christ but in a superficial, intellectual way. I never wondered, *Why did God make me?* Everything is made for a purpose—a watch, a car, a TV. But me? I never thought about it.

But now, at this camp, when Larry spoke to me about my cousin, it hit me that I might not be a Christian either.

Why did it hit me then and never before? I suppose you would say the Holy Spirit had never singled me out. In "natural" terms, I saw the contrast between these young people and me. *I saw that God was real to them.* These were my peers. And if *they* believed in Christ. . . .

I think that's what finally got through to me. Something was real to them. They were different. Finally, after all the years of exposure to the things of God, after all my mother's pleading letters and prayers, I could see the contrast between their lives and mine.

Anyway, Larry Doyle, formerly a tough gang leader in New York City, looked at me and said, "You don't think you're a Christian? Look . . . I want to see you down on the beach tomorrow afternoon."

I met him the next day. We sat on some high rocks under the trees above beautiful Schroon Lake. It was a gorgeous summer day. A breeze gently rustled the leaves above us, and in a piercing blue sky, puffy clouds drifted like boats. Larry began to talk with me about God. He hit me right between the eyes with the Truth.

One thing in particular stopped me cold in my tracks: He said, "*It's possible for you to know God like you know your best friend.*"

I said, "Boy . . . if that's possible, then I would really like to know God."

"That *is* possible . . . ," he replied, not letting me off the hook.

The thought amazed me—the possibility of knowing the God of the universe personally. Up until this time, as far as I was concerned, God was out there, someplace beyond Pluto.

I had been living my life the way I wanted to, as much as

possible, and God wasn't a consideration or part of the picture. I enjoyed doing my own thing.

Larry mentioned something else that impressed me. He told me God had made me for a purpose. The thought had never crossed my mind. Why *had* God made me? That seemed to be a very important question. For if I could know why God made me, and I were to begin to fulfill that purpose, then life would take on real meaning and I would be supremely happy.

So the question now was this: What was His purpose for me? Larry went on: "Ike, what does God want from us, more than anything else? Our time . . . our money . . . our lives? What do *we* want from our families more than anything else?"

I didn't quite know what he was getting at.

"Jesus gave us the answer," he said, "in Matthew twenty-two, verses thirty-seven and thirty-eight. Some lawyers were trying to test Him, and they asked, 'Which is the most important commandment? What's the most important thing in life?' And Jesus answered them, 'Each one of us is "to love God with all our heart, soul and mind. This is the first and greatest commandment." ' "

Here it was—the answer to the deepest philosophical questions of all the ages: *I had been created to love God; Jesus Christ Himself had said so.* And yet, for almost twenty-one years I did not know that. What's more, I couldn't remember anyone ever telling me this before. If they did, it went over my head—a dead lesson that never came alive for me.

It was odd. For the previous two years I had been living with my wonderful Christian mother, whom I was trying to learn to love again. In spite of all the suffering in her life—her husband's premature death, the loss of her health, and having her children taken away for ten years—she had come forth as pure gold. Mother had a very intimate relationship with God; yet somehow, I had been blind to the fact that this could ever be a possibility for me.

I sat there on the rocks, listening to Larry Doyle, drinking it all in. He encouraged me to give God a chance in my life. He challenged me that when I returned home I should read a chapter of the Gospel of John every night before I went to bed.

I promised I would, but I told him I felt the Bible had too many contradictions.

With that, he handed me the Bible and said, "Is that so? Here . . . show them to me."

I stared at the leather-bound book and said sheepishly, "You know, Larry, I . . . I really don't know what's in there. Uh . . . I've only heard other people say there are contradictions in there. . . ."

The truth was I had never studied the Bible and only on rare occasions as an adolescent had I ever even read parts of it. The few times I had read the Bible, I hadn't really understood it, and I told that to Larry. He then shared with me that this was the job of the Holy Spirit—to give understanding to those who would read the Scriptures.

The Holy Ghost . . . as a teenager, I had repeated the formula many times in church: "In the name of the Father, and of the Son, and of the Holy Ghost. Amen." Who in the world was the Holy Ghost? I was beginning to find out. . . .

"Ike, when you read the Bible, *why* did you read it?" Larry asked.

"Because I saw my mother reading it when I was a child," I replied, "and so I thought it was a good Book."

He smiled. "Ike, even though your motives were good, they were still wrong."

"What do you mean, my motives were wrong?"

"The right reason to read the Bible is that we might come to know God personally. *This* is the reason God has given us the Bible . . . to reveal Himself and His plan for our lives to us. And most important, to reveal His love for us.

"Ike," he continued, "when you go home, before you read the Bible, you should first pray this little prayer: 'God, please, as I read Your Word, reveal Yourself to me. I really want to know You.' "

Then Larry got down to cases. He explained the plan of salvation to me in clear terms: I was a sinner. He argued persuasively that if the greatest commandment was to love God with all my heart, then the greatest sin would be *not* to love Him. And I was guilty of not loving God. So Jesus Christ had to die for *me,* for *my* sin.

I had to admit my guilt, Larry said. Then I had to accept Christ by faith alone. If I did, I would become a Christian, assured of a place in heaven.

"Ike," he concluded, "you've got everything to gain and nothing to lose. Why don't you make this decision and invite Jesus Christ to come into your life?"

I thought I understood the things he had been telling me, but it was heavy, heavy stuff. It was a big step, making this kind of life-changing decision. I wasn't sure I should. Yet . . . it all seemed so . . . logical.

Larry Doyle was forceful—very strong, very persuasive. Finally I said, "All right . . . I'll do it."

Sitting there by that beautiful lake, under the sky of piercing blue with its drifting clouds, we bowed our heads and Larry led me in prayer.

"Jesus," I repeated after him, "I'm a sinner, and I want You to come into my life. You've given Your life for me, and now I give my life back to You."

In a way, I did this to get Larry off my back . . . but not totally. *I was going to give God a chance . . . I was going to try to get to know Him.*

8. A New Creature

Therefore if any man be in Christ, he is a new creature: old things are passed away; behold, all things are become new.

2 Corinthians 5:17 KJV

Up until this time, God had been a stranger to me. In retrospect, even though he pushed me, I can never thank Larry Doyle enough for his persistence and his love for me—and more important, for the Lord. This decision was to change the entire course of my life.

At the time, I hardly knew what my decision for Christ was all about. But because I had accepted the Lord and shone in sports, I was to give my testimony on the radio that Saturday evening, at our youth rally.

Mother was listening to the radio at home, and she heard me give my testimony. She was thrilled to pieces. I think of all the years she had prayed for Al and me, all the tears she must have shed. Finally, it had all come to fruition.

I returned home and started reading my Bible every day, as I had promised. And as Larry had instructed me, prayed: "Lord, I want You to reveal Yourself to me."

I started out reading the first chapter of John. I didn't understand much of it, and I had some difficulty reading from the beautiful old King James Version.

There was another more serious problem. Though I sincerely wanted to know God, I found I couldn't believe in the miracles recorded in the Bible.

How could God make everything from nothing? How could Jesus walk on the water . . . or feed five thousand men (plus women and children) from a few loaves and fishes? How could

He be raised from the dead? How could Jesus be God? How could Jonah be swallowed by a big fish and live?

Now, I had believed all these things at Bonnie Brae. I had written my senior essay on the life of Christ (which, by the way, I had copied from Classic Comics).

But now, as an adult, when I was confronted by the age-old question, "Who is this Man, Jesus Christ?" I had grave doubts. *Could He,* I wondered, *really be God? Why, He was a kid like me who grew up in a little village. And He tells His buddies, "Hey . . . I'm God"?*

Well, as I read, I found more and more that I couldn't believe it. And I *wanted* to believe it! What was happening? Belief—even the little I had before my conversion—was vanishing. Slowly but surely, I was becoming . . . an atheist.

I didn't want to upset Mother, so I continued going to church. And I continued to read John's Gospel, pray, and memorize Bible verses, but only because I had promised Larry I would. I said nothing of my inner struggles to anyone.

Things got worse. Not only did I find I could no longer believe in miracles, *I no longer believed in Jesus.* Finally, *I no longer believed there was a God.*

The Bible, I decided, was a collection of fairy tales. There was no Creator. It all "just happened." It was a cosmic accident. *I* was a cosmic accident. And how could I pray to God before reading the Bible when He no longer existed?

Yet strangely, I continued to read it . . . what a dilemma! I don't know how long this state of affairs lasted—maybe a month or two.

Then slowly, as I continued to read the Bible, things began to change. Until now, my thoughts had been in a steady downward spiral. Unaccountably, the spiral now began to reverse itself and was on an upward climb toward understanding and acceptance. In retrospect, I can only say it was the influence of the Holy Spirit, shedding His light as I studied God's Word. What had Larry said: something about it being the job of the Holy Spirit to give us understanding, if we would read the Word.

I came to see that there is so much order in the universe, from the distant galaxies to our own solar system to the tiny atom. There is order and design in everything, from the largest to the smallest. My watch (I observed) didn't accidentally "happen": There was a designer, a creator—the watchmaker. And it was made for a purpose: to tell time.

I saw there is a cause for every effect. *Therefore,* I reasoned, *I am not an accident . . . I was made by a loving Creator for a purpose.* Furthermore, this Creator had sent His Son to our planet. I had doubted and foolishly declared that Jesus had never existed. Yet Jesus Christ was not only in the Bible but also in the encyclopedias and all the secular history books, as far back as Josephus, a Jewish historian and contemporary of Christ, who wrote briefly about Him, as did Tacitus, a pagan Roman historian.

I was pondering all this in July and August of 1952. I thought, *Why, 1952 A.D.—1,952 years after His birth.* I marveled at that fact: *The world even reckons time according to this man Jesus!*

It was all making sense. The pieces were fitting together. Then I thought of something else: Because there was so much that is good in the world, there has to be a Source of it all: *God.* At the same time, there is so much evil in the world, there has to be a source for that also.

Thus, I became aware of a real devil: Satan, as he is called in the Bible. I used to think he was a funny guy with a pitchfork in a little red suit. But Jesus spoke about him in the Bible as a very real, powerful, and evil person—the enemy of God.

I realized what had happened when I briefly became an atheist: It was Satan himself who instigated my doubts, seeking to keep me out of the family of God. And he almost did. But as the Bible says, ". . . greater is he [God] that is in you, than he [Satan] that is in the world" (1 John 4:4 KJV).

So it was that Satan departed and the Holy Spirit began to open my eyes to the truth of God. I began to understand Scripture.

I was beginning to believe . . . to understand spiritual truth. Finally, I had to tell myself, *Now, Jesus was either a liar, or crazy, or He really was who He said He was.*

I had finally come to know Him!

In my high school years, I knew clergymen who were so interested in me and my future that they were prepared to pay my way through college and seminary. They saw to it that I went to church conferences and church camps. *Yet never did any of them tell me I could know God personally, as I knew my best friend.*

Now Jesus was not only my best friend; He was also my Master. I knew I had been created to love God and serve Him. Like the Apostle Paul, my question now was, "Lord, what do You want me to do?"

That September, I enrolled in the Newark Evening Bible School. On an alternate night, I began attending Bible classes at Hawthorne Gospel Church. I couldn't get enough of God's Word! And every Saturday night, I went into Manhattan to Jack Wyrtzen's Times Square Rally.

It wasn't all roses. Just after I committed myself to the Lord, Mother told me something that rubbed me the wrong way.

I was having a terrible time, financially. I had just cashed in my penny bank that I had been saving for years, and my Scottish pounds and shillings. I was also working those two jobs . . . and with all that, I still couldn't make ends meet. It wasn't easy supporting the three of us on my meager salary of thirty dollars a week.

And what was Mother's answer to the financial crunch?

"Izat," she said sweetly, "you need to tithe."

"Mother," I replied, upset, "what in the world are you talking about? Me? *Tithe?* Why, I can't even pay my bills! I just cashed everything in. That's ridiculous!"

"Why don't you take these verses," she replied calmly, "and go in your room and study them?"

She gave me a number of verses, including the famous Malachi 3:10 (KJV):

> *Bring ye all the tithes into the storehouse, that there may be meat in mine house, and prove me now herewith, saith the Lord of hosts, if I will not open you the windows of heaven, and pour you out a blessing, that there shall not be room enough to receive it.*

I studied those verses and prayed over them. Then I came out of my room and said to Mother, "Boy . . . that's really something

. . . God says He's going to bless you if you tithe. I'm going to give it a try and take that ten percent off, as soon as I get my paycheck."

And I did.

Things began to happen: Out of the blue, I got a check in the mail. Somebody had sent me a gift of money.

What a coincidence, I thought. *Coincidence, nothing!* I chided myself. *That's exactly what God said He would do!*

During this crunch, unexpected money was to come to me three or four times.

I began to think of ways to make extra money. I asked my boss at Esso if he would mind if I brought in some of Auntie's delicious gingerbread and special ice tea to sell during coffee breaks. He said no, go ahead.

And people just loved them. I was making thirty dollars a week salary—and soon I was doubling my income, making another thirty dollars on coffee breaks! I felt God had given me the idea of selling food, inspiring my initiative, to bless me. Because of my tithing, God was supplying my needs. This was a tangible, measurable way in which I could see that He was fulfilling His promises in the Bible.

And though I was in the prime of my young manhood, God now gave me control over my impulses. He cleaned up my mind and my mouth.

Jack Wyrtzen helped. He emphasized the story of Joseph in the Bible. Day after day, Joseph resisted the temptation of Potiphar's wife (Genesis 39). He kept his purity and did not betray his master or his God. In sad contrast was the story of David, "a man after God's own heart," who succumbed to adultery and murder, and because of his sin had a sword run through his entire family (2 Samuel 11 and following). God used these examples to show me I really had to keep myself pure, and that it was possible. Hearing Jack Wyrtzen preach week after week, as well as receiving the sound counsel of Christian friends, helped reinforce my good resolves.

Soon after my conversion, I found I was becoming restless in my job at Esso. Almost right away I was asking an important question: *Well, Lord, what do You want me to do with my life?* My desire was to go into full-time Christian service, but with Mother and Auntie to take care of, I felt I couldn't.

My thoughts were turning more and more to Bonnie Brae. It wasn't the gentle green hills and sloping pastures, the wide lawns and playing fields, or the four cottages that were drawing me. It was the boys . . . a whole new generation of lonely, hurting kids, so full of sadness and pain. *They needed Jesus.*

I had needed Jesus when I was there, and somehow I had missed out on Him. If only I had known Him back then, when I was missing Mother so much, when I was facing the daily grind, the loveless atmosphere, the bullying, Jesus would have comforted me. When my dear mother couldn't provide for me, He would have taken me up.

If only I had been told about Him. But with all the discipline and training, churchgoing and lip service reverence for God, I never knew Him back then.

So now the Lord was telling me in my heart and mind, as clearly as if He had come down bodily to speak the words: *I want you to go back to Bonnie Brae and tell those boys about Me.*

"But how can I do that, Lord," I asked, "with Mother and Auntie to care for?" In obedience to His leading, I applied for a job as housefather at the farm and was accepted. I would be going back. . . .

So within a year of my conversion—June 1953—I handed in my resignation at Esso and prepared to move Mother and Auntie to live with a friend in Millington, to be near me. Before I left Esso, my friends there had a nice going-away party for me and gave me a beautiful 35mm camera. I would miss them, but with joy and anticipation I prepared to return to the farm to begin a new chapter in my life.

Mother and Auntie were glad about the move, too. Mother was particularly excited that I was going back to tell the kids about the Lord.

I was on Cloud 9. I may have missed out, but what a joy it would be to share Jesus with this new crop of kids. I could hardly wait. . . .

9. Into the Harvest

I heard the voice of the Lord, saying, Whom shall I send, and who will go for us? Then said I, Here am I; send me.

Isaiah 6:8 KJV

I was made housefather at Osborne Cottage. The administration preferred couples, but it was a stopgap situation. I was the only single houseparent covering the four cottages.

Charlie Group, our former director, had left. The new director was Warren Waters. Although we differed in our religious beliefs, I don't think I've ever met a better man than Warren. It was a privilege to know him and work for him.

For the next three years I had real freedom to share with the boys. The first two years I was at Osborne, and the third year I was a relief houseparent.

Each evening we'd have devotions and I would share God's Word with the boys. I tried not to preach at them; it would have turned them off. But they needed instruction. For instance, stealing had always been a problem among the kids. So I taught them that honesty makes sense: Everyone needs to work to earn his own money, so he can have self-respect and can help others, rather than steal from them. Without sounding pious, I told them God wanted them to respect the other person's rights and that He ultimately was the One who would supply their needs.

I was also scoutmaster at this time, so I could tie the Scout Oath—"A Scout is honest, trustworthy, thrifty, brave, clean, and reverent"—to scriptural principles.

With twenty-one kids under my supervision, there were always arguments and fights; these boys were just as hurt and angry as we had been, ten years before. So I had plenty of opportunity to mediate, to defuse hostility and jealousy—and to remind them that Jesus told us we were to "love one another, as He loves us" (*see* John 13:34).

I was very careful; I sought God's wisdom in dealing with the kids, because if every time I talked to the boys about doing wrong I mentioned Jesus, after a while the kids would have been turned off to Him, "because He spoils all our fun." So I tried to be sensitive and ask myself, *Is this the right time to bring Jesus into the situation?*

Only once was money stolen from my room, although I would leave the cottage money box right out on my dresser, to show the kids I trusted them. We talked so much about the necessity of honesty that they could walk in and out of my room and would never think of touching that seventy dollars.

But one day, fifteen dollars was gone. Following my policy when there was a theft, I called the kids together and gave them a serious talk about the importance of honesty. Then I had the kids come into my room to see me, one at a time. They knew what to expect: They were to tell me, "Yes, I did it," or "No, I didn't do it," with no explanations. It took only about fifteen to thirty seconds for each boy.

If no one confessed, I'd have the boys come in individually a second time, and then they would be free to tell me if they knew who had done it, since the thief wasn't being honest.

On this particular occasion, the boy who stole the money came clean the first time around (which was what usually happened). He broke down and cried.

"Now, calm down," I told him. "It's serious, but it's not the end of the world. Get back out there. If you're in here too long, the other guys will suspect you did it. I'll see you later and we'll talk about it."

He was a nice, sensitive lad, and this was something totally out of character for him. So I asked him later, with some exasperation, "Gary, why in the world did you do it?"

"Somebody stole the money I was saving to buy a present for my sister . . . for her birthday." His lower lip began to twitch. "So . . . so, I h-h-had to take the money from your room. I didn't take it all . . . only what they stole from me!"

"Well, Gary, the Lord can help us in situations like this. If you had told me, first I would have tried to help you . . . we'd have found the guy who stole from you."

"I . . . I'm sorry," he said, "I won't do it again, honest!"

"I know you won't, Gary," I said. "Now run along. And don't say anything to anybody about this. Okay?"

Gary never stole anything again.

There was a boy who was a real thief, though—a pro. His father had taught him how to do it. He'd steal money out of the teachers' purses at public school. Of course he stole at the cottage, too.

One time, after he had been caught at school, I asked him, "Lenny, how come you never steal from me? The cottage money is always out in plain sight. . . ."

"Because I like you, Pop," he replied. "I don't steal from people I like."

"What do you do with the money? You never seem to have any on you."

He shifted his weight from one foot to the other and looked off into space. "I buy stuff for my friends . . . candy and cake and comics and stuff. . . ."

Lenny was stealing to buy friendship. He felt so worthless he thought nobody would like him unless he "bought" them.

I tried to tell him he didn't have to do that; the kind of friends you have to buy aren't worth much anyway. I told him if he'd try being nice to other boys, they just might be nice back. Rather than waiting for someone to befriend him, he needed to take the first step and be a friend to someone else. And then he might get some *real* friends.

I must admit I did a lot of what some people today might call "brainwashing" through rules, repetition, and example. But it is our responsibility as parents and caretakers to pass our values on to our children. I was regularly sharing Christian principles *before* an offense was committed. I made it a point to tell them in advance what was going to happen. This way they could prepare their minds and set their priorities. I'd say, "Kids . . . when we're together, if it's worktime, we work; we don't play.

If it's playtime, that's when we play; we don't work! So if you're playing and it's worktime, you're out of line. We don't do that." With repetition and consistency, they got the picture.

I kept repeating about the stealing and the bullying and many other things. But especially the bullying. . . .

"Look, guys," I'd say, "I used to get beat up by older guys. And I *hated* it. No one likes it . . . do you want somebody to beat up on you? Do *you* like it when somebody hits you, bullies you?"

Of course there were guys who were chronic toughies and liars, very unhappy, disturbed kids. I had one kid who, every time I walked into the room, would do something out of line, just to get my attention. He was so starved for somebody to care.

"Joey . . . stop poking Denny!" I'd say, and he'd stop and be good as gold. Yet the next time it would be something else, because all the attention you could give this boy would never satisfy that hunger he had to be loved.

When kids don't get the love and physical affection they need the first year of their lives—which is absolutely critical to normal development—there is no real parental bonding. So the children become insecure and anxious. They are restless, like butterflies, going from flower to flower—never getting enough love—unless and until God begins to deal with them, making them feel valued and loved, through Christ.

About this time, something happened that was quite significant, though I didn't realize it at the time. For a number of years I had a real desire to return to Scotland to visit my relatives. While I was working at the farm, my grandmother in Scotland sent me some money for that very purpose.

So in 1955, eighteen years after coming to this country, I was finally able to return to the land of my birth. It was an exciting time. I traveled alone, sailing over on the *Queen Mary* and returning on the *Queen Elizabeth* three weeks later.

It was great to be able to visit my relatives and the scenes of my early childhood. And what a time I had getting reacquainted with cousins, aunts, and uncles—and my grandparents.

Grandma Keay was now eighty-four years old but still spry, doing all the cooking. She was very much the matriarch of the Keay clan.

I wanted to know about my father and about his death. Mother had always been rather vague about the details of the tragic accident.

For instance, Mother had given me the impression that my dad had died in a hunting accident. I had imagined it was while tramping through the Highlands. But Grandma said he was only "hunting" rats when it happened. She took me out to one of the barns behind the main farmhouse, where the accident had actually occurred. She pointed to the very spot where she had found him.

I got a peculiar feeling, looking at that bit of dingy, nondescript floor, realizing that this was where my father's life had ended. It was a sober moment.

"And your father didn't kill himself, either!" Grandma suddenly said defensively.

I looked at her, not knowing how to respond to this outlandish statement, but said to myself, *Well, I know he didn't and nobody ever said he did. . . .*

My poor grandmother! She had seen two other sons die of natural causes, and then my father. And she was the one who had found his body. What a terrible thing to have witnessed. It was clear the horror of that day had stayed with her all those years.

I was so thankful to have been able to visit my grandparents for what was to be the last time on earth. Grandpa died four years later at eighty-five, and Grandma died thirteen years later at ninety-seven—both of them "full of years and honors."

I returned to Bonnie Brae and continued to work with the boys. Because of their emotional problems, some of them had trouble learning. Although bedtime was nine o'clock, I'd stay up with some kids until ten or eleven, going over their assignments. No scholar myself, I knew what they were going through.

Just as my head was about to hit the table from exhaustion, one of them would suddenly say, "Oh . . . hey, Pop, I see what that means!" I'd see the light in his face and eyes, the sheer pleasure of discovery and understanding.

Bedtime is a golden time for children: *This is probably the most important time of the day.* At Bonnie Brae, it sometimes seemed it could go on until morning. The boys would get into bed and I would go around to all twenty-one of them, one at a time, for a talk, a hug, and a kiss. Then I'd read to them for fifteen or twenty minutes from a Christian adventure book.

Before I turned the light out, those who were still awake would say, "Pop . . . give me another hug." And I'd give each one of them one more big hug and a kiss. Oh, how they needed that love and affection! I could remember all too well the lonely nights when I was a Bonnie Brae boy, with no one to tuck me in.

About this time, February 1956, five Protestant missionaries were murdered by the Auca Indians in the jungles of Ecuador, South America. The incident made international headlines. I followed every word of it in the newspapers and on radio and television. That event had a major bearing on my future.

Since my conversion, I had wanted to prepare myself for full-time Christian service. When those five young men were martyred, I prayed, "Lord I want to take the place of one of those missionaries."

But at the time, I was a "missionary" to the boys at Bonnie Brae. In all my nurturing of those kids, I was always conscious of their need to know the Lord Jesus. Although I was careful not to put pressure on any of them, occasionally a boy would accept the Lord, and what a joy that was!

Yet, as low-keyed as I tried to be in presenting Jesus to those boys who needed Him so badly, my sharing with them eventually led to my undoing.

By this time (the mid-1950s), to Bonnie Brae's credit, psychiatrists and counselors had been brought in to work with the boys, many of whom had emotional problems. But when a boy would tell one of the counselors he had accepted the Lord, it wasn't appreciated.

Finally, the counselors went to Mr. Waters and complained. He called me to his office with a caseworker and told me, "Ike, you know I'm in sympathy with the fact that you're a devout Christian. But some of the staff are disturbed that you are indoctrinating the boys into evangelical Christianity.

"Although we're a private institution," he continued, "we have boys of all faiths here. The counselors don't feel it's . . . uh, proper for us to teach them only one way. So, I have to tell you that from now on, the only things in the way of religion that you can teach the boys are the Twenty-Third Psalm and the Lord's Prayer. Nothing else. I'm really sorry."

The caseworker added, "We all have our private religious convictions, Ike, but quite frankly, we feel it isn't healthy to be constantly harping on religion to impressionable boys."

"I'm sorry, but I have to disagree," I said. "When I was here as a boy, no one ever told me that God loved me or that He would be my Friend. And I needed that. These boys need that.

"We were created to love God . . . and it's only Jesus who can bring us into a proper relationship with God. These kids are so hurt and damaged. He's the *real* Answer . . . the One who can really change their lives . . . give them healing and wholeness! Please don't deny them that!"

"We're sorry," she said, with an edge of impatience, "you *cannot* continue to proselytize the boys."

"If you're telling me I can't tell these kids about Jesus," I said, my voice shaking with emotion, "and . . . if I can't even teach them Bible verses . . . well, I'm sorry, but I'm not going to be able to stay here." And I meant it. I didn't feel I could stay on and go against their authority.

As much as I loved those kids, I knew I couldn't do them any lasting good unless I could share the love of Jesus with them.

With the deaths of those five missionaries, and now my having to leave Bonnie Brae, I sensed that God was preparing me for the next chapter of my life.

While all this was going on, my brother, Al, who was now married and leaving the air force after six years of duty, said that he and his wife would like to take care of Mother for a while. Al knew about my long-standing desire to attend college.

"Look, Ike," he said, "we'll take Mother now, and you can do what you always wanted to do."

"I can't let you do that, Al," I replied. "You'll be in college, too . . . and you and Cheryl are expecting a baby."

"You've taken care of Mother for six years now!" he protested. "She's my mother, too; she's just as much my responsibility as yours! And as far as our having the baby . . . well, Mother will be a big help to Cheryl. Let's not argue about it. Okay?"

So it was decided. I asked Uncle Norman if he could take Auntie into his home. He and Aunt Louise said sure, they'd be happy to.

It seemed the doors were opening. After all those years, finally, I would be able to go to school.

And what of Mother? She was delighted about my being able to go to Bible college. (I had decided on Moody Bible Institute in Chicago.) This was what she had always wanted for me—to think, her son would be a missionary, spreading God's Word! Mother felt her deepest prayers had been answered.

In early September, I packed everything I owned (which wasn't much) in my old car, bade good-bye to Bonnie Brae and my friends at Millington Baptist Church, and left New Jersey, heading west toward Illinois . . . and Moody Bible Institute. At last I was about to begin my formal education in preparation to serve the Lord!

Thank You, Father, and thank You, Jesus. I am ready. . . .

10. Moody

Study to shew thyself approved unto God, a workman that needeth not to be ashamed, rightly dividing the word of truth.

2 Timothy 2:15 KJV

Often referred to as the "West Point of Christian training," Moody Bible Institute was founded in 1887 by the famous nineteenth-century evangelist Dwight L. Moody. As befits an institution dedicated to the spread of the Gospel among men of all classes, Moody is located in downtown Chicago, which is about as inner-city as you can get. Directly across from our dormitories were seedy bars where drugs were dealt; on the streets prostitutes openly plied their trade.

Yet, in spite of its surroundings, to me Moody was a little bit of heaven on earth. I had been out of school more than six years when I began my studies there in the fall of 1956. And although in high school I had never been keen on books and studying, since becoming a committed Christian I had an insatiable hunger to learn.

Added to this remarkable change was the fact that I was an older student of twenty-five. Most of the other freshmen were eighteen-year-olds just out of high school. I had been out in the world, supporting a family of three; I had matured and was serious about life. I knew how tough it was out there. So I now appreciated the value of learning—particularly learning about the things of God. I had lost so many precious years; I had no time to waste.

So I plunged into my studies eagerly. Not that I was a whiz by any means. I still had only average intelligence and had to plod along; nothing came easy to me. I had to work twice as hard as the younger, brighter students.

Then, too, my study habits had rusted. I had to relearn the

discipline of taking notes in class and applying myself to my books in a sustained, organized way. It wasn't easy. But I didn't mind . . . *I felt I just couldn't learn enough!*

I loved all my classes. That first semester we all had to take English, our only secular subject. You see, Dwight L. Moody, our founder, began life as a shoe salesman, without much formal education. And although he was one of the most powerful evangelists of his day, by his own admission he murdered the English language. So he believed that a Christian should be able to speak clearly and write properly in presenting the Gospel of Christ.

In high school I had never grasped the basic concepts of English grammar. But before I left for Moody, a dear friend gave me some elementary school English books. So there I was, in college, going back to those simple children's books and picking up the basics again—and getting *A*s in English!

I also had courses such as Old Testament, World Missions, and Personal Evangelism. It was a somewhat accelerated three-year course; the first two semesters were each regarded as a year.

Students were not allowed to work that first semester, and although things were tight for me financially, I managed. The situation was certainly made much better by the fact that no student at Moody had ever been charged tuition, thanks to its many donors.

By the second semester, however, things began to get really rough, both in my studies and finances. For example, I was taking a course in New Testament Greek. There was a whole new alphabet to learn! To get it into my head was like pounding through concrete. Many kids failed that course. But tough as it was, I loved it. And it helped that we had an excellent professor, Dr. Kenneth (Skipper) Weust, a world-famous Greek scholar. To think that I would someday be able to read the New Testament in the original language!

Studies, however, weren't my main problem. By the second semester my nest egg was gone, so I had to take a job in a hardware store, working twenty hours a week, in addition to my full class load. And I was still just squeaking by.

Mother was aware of my situation. "Don't get discouraged," she wrote. "You will get spiritual aid soon. Jesus never fails. We may fail Him, but He remains faithful." She gave her widow's mite to help me, but she and I both knew the Lord would provide. And He did, in remarkable ways, just as He had when I began tithing.

I remember when I didn't have even ten cents to buy a bar of soap. I got down on my knees and prayed, "Lord, You have promised that You would supply my every need, and I need ten cents for a bar of soap. Thank You."

An inner voice urged, *Check your pants pockets again.* I had already gone through them carefully, but I was obedient to His command. Getting up, I checked all my pockets again. In the top of a pocket I found a dime, wedged in a corner. There was my bar of soap—and there I was, a "little child," asking my Heavenly Father for the necessities of life.

Another time, I was driving one of our Moody school buses and I needed a chauffeur's license, which cost $5.00 (a lot of money to me). I checked my wallet and pants and found $3.20. I still needed a $1.80.

You may be asking, "Why didn't he just borrow the money from a friend?" A few years earlier, I had made a promise to the Lord that I would ask only Him to supply my needs. Now I needed $1.80. So once again I got on my knees. This time He said, *Go get your penny bank.*

I poured all my pennies on the bed and began counting. You guessed it: *exactly 180 pennies.* If God could count the hairs on my head, it was no problem for Him to provide the exact number of pennies I needed!

But it was a grind. I had absolutely no time for dating, relaxation, or fun. In fact, I slept only about three hours a night. Every night, I would go to bed at 10:30 P.M. and get up at 2:00 A.M. to study, because it took me so long to learn what other students absorbed easily.

Knowing how difficult it was to get up at that hour, I rigged up a Rube Goldberg device to help me: I attached a piece of string to the pull chain of my overhead light bulb and tied it to the headboard of my bed. Then I took my metal wastepaper basket and put my alarm clock inside the can, so that when the bell went off it would vibrate the basket and make a loud, unpleasant noise. I also kept a wet washrag on the floor next to the can.

As soon as I heard the clock rattling in the can, I hit the string with my arm, which turned the light on. Then I turned the alarm off and grabbed the wet washrag and wiped my face—all in one motion. I was ready to go.

My next-door roommate saw that my system worked and asked if I would help him get up early, too. I was glad to oblige. We got to know each other, and I found out he was having some serious problems with his fiancée.

Craig's fiancée was a pretty, vivacious brunette with cute round cheeks. Her name was Carolyn.

They would try to get me to double-date with them, but I really wasn't interested in girls at the time. I was at Moody to study; it was that simple.

Craig would come back from his dates with Carolyn all upset and out of sorts. The problem, he said, was that she was too outspoken and strong-willed. If he suggested something, she would want to do something else.

"You've got to be stronger and start making more decisions," I had told him. "She *expects* you to be the leader in this relationship."

Things didn't seem to be getting any better, so Craig asked me to have a talk with Carolyn. We met in the sweetshop one afternoon. As she sat there sipping a Coke, I noticed once again that she was a very sweet girl.

Then I began to explain to her what Craig's frustrations were. "Carolyn, you're such a strong person by nature; I don't think you realize it. You automatically control situations by being so outgoing and outspoken. Craig is more the quiet type; you have to give him more of a chance to lead, or he'll get discouraged."

Although I knew Carolyn respected my opinion, I wasn't sure

what her reaction would be to my suggestions about their relationship. But she was very positive and sweet about it all. She admitted she was perhaps a bit too strong-willed and impulsive. She thanked me for my concern and said she appreciated it. She promised to try to let Craig take the lead and to be more sensitive to his feelings.

Mother's letters were full of news of Al, our family back in New Jersey, and much spiritual encouragement. Occasionally she mentioned her health, which was a continuing problem:

> I had another cold that didn't last too long, although at times I don't feel too good. But I can't let that get me down. Good or bad, I have a Lord to glorify. And so long as I have a breath I'll sing His praises. No matter if my chest is giving way. It gives me great consolation to pick up my hymnbook and sing some of the lovely hymns: "Jesus, Oh How Sweet Thy Name," "Higher Ground," "Our Great Saviour." One sings in all conditions—good and bad. . . . Jesus Christ is the Way, Jesus Christ is the Truth, Jesus Christ is the Life, and He is mine, mine, mine. . . .

During my first semester at Moody, though, I noticed that the return address on Mother's letters changed. I knew Al had been transferred from Spokane to Rapid City, South Dakota, and Mother had gone with Cheryl and him. But why would her address now be different from theirs?

When I went out to visit the family that Christmas I found out. Cheryl and her parents objected to Mother living with Al and her. They all felt it was an imposition on Cheryl who, after all, was a new bride with adjustments to make. So, within a few weeks of moving to Rapid City, Al had gotten Mother her own small apartment.

Al was torn between his wife and his duty to his ailing mother.

"I took Mother because you had been shouldering all the responsibility," he said, "I guess I was naive . . . I guess I thought that once I was married, living with me might be easier for Mother . . . and she tried so hard. But if she was darning my socks, Cheryl would get annoyed—well, you know how Mother cared for us . . . it made Cheryl feel a little insecure.

"And even when we were in Spokane—I hate to say it, Ike—I think Mother was beginning to deteriorate mentally. She imagined the doctors were plotting to take her back to the hospital. And she'd be singing hymns in the middle of the night. . . ."

As he talked, I was thinking about that letter in which she mentioned the hymns. I hadn't known Mother was waking them up during the night. . . .

Anyway, I was really hurting over the way things had turned out, so I decided I would drop out of school and take Mother again.

But Al wouldn't hear of it. He wanted to give things a bit longer. Besides, he said, Mother was all settled in now, in her own little place. And as for her health, he argued that she was a permanent invalid and she wasn't going to improve dramatically, no matter where she was.

Mother insisted she was going to be just fine and that what would please her the most would be seeing me back in school. So I compromised with her: I would complete the next semester and then drop out the following summer, to care for her once again.

Al promised to keep me informed.

On April 18, a beautiful spring day, I got the call from Al. Mother had had a massive heart attack. She was in intensive care. Every hair stood up on my body. "Lord, there's no way You can take my mother!" It wasn't a prayer; it was a demand.

In Rapid City, Al had just been mustered out of the air force as a first lieutenant. With Cheryl and Mother, he was on his way back to Spokane to establish a new home and begin his studies at the University of Washington on the GI Bill.

They had been driving through Montana when it happened. After only one day on the road, Mother hadn't been able to get up the next morning. Al thought the high elevation may have brought it on. She was in a hospital in a small Indian town.

"I'm coming out, Al," I said.

"No, don't. Ike," he said, his voice husky, "the doctor said her chances of living through the night aren't worth a plugged nickel."

"I'm coming anyway."

I knew by the time I drove out there she might be dead. She *couldn't* die . . . not Mother. There was so much I wanted to do for her yet. "God," I prayed, "don't you dare take my mother! Don't You *dare!*"

If I were going to go at all, I'd have to fly . . . but I had no money. Then the Lord stepped in: When word got around campus, my friends took up a collection for my plane ticket. What a wonderful bunch of people they were—and what an unfailing Lord we have!

But all the way out on that twelve-hundred-mile flight, one sentence pounded in my heart and brain: *God, don't You dare take my mother! Don't You dare take my mother!*

I argued with Him: *Lord, I already said I was going to drop out of school this summer to take care of her! Lord, after You, she's my first responsibility!*

Al met me at the airport, encouraged. "Ike . . . Mother's improved greatly. The doctors can't understand the change!"

The Lord had heard my cry . . . my eyes welled up with tears of praise. I prayed aloud right there in the car: "Oh, thank You, Jesus! Thank You!" I was feeling a bit ashamed that I had castigated God all the way out there. But I knew He understood. Our God is so gracious and kind, particularly when His children are hurting.

We drove to a small hospital. It was true: Mother was much improved. The doctors were amazed, but they told Al and me that she'd be in the hospital at least six weeks.

I was so grateful to the Lord for having spared her. She was very weak, of course, but Al said she looked so much better than she had a day earlier.

Mother was so glad to see me. I sat with her and held her hand. We prayed. . . .

The next day I took a bus back to Chicago to pack up my things and drive back out to Montana to be with Mother. School was out of the question right now. I would drop out. And there would be the matter of the hospital bill. I had no money, and Al and Cheryl had a baby on the way.

At least six weeks, the doctors had said. The hospital bill was going to be sky-high. But Mother was going to live. That was all that mattered.

Still, it was an emotional time for me, having to leave all my friends and Moody. I had grown so much, spiritually. Before I left, I went over to the bookstore to buy a lot of books that were on sale, so I could at least do some reading. While I was in Montana I would be working in the oil fields at a dollar an hour, but I was also going to be a missionary to the Native Americans at a nearby reservation. I wanted to be prepared.

By the time I got back out to Montana on April 27, ten days after her heart attack, Mother had taken a turn for the worse. I was alarmed at the change in her.

She was in an oxygen tent. Her speech was garbled and unclear.

After I left intensive care, Al said, "Ike, Cheryl and I are going to have to go on. We can't stay any longer, with her pregnant. The doctor says Mother could stay like this for weeks. You'd better find a place to rent and unload your stuff. . . ."

Instead I went into our motel bathroom, which was the only place I could get alone to pray. I knelt down by the toilet. My heart was breaking.

"Lord," I began, "You just *cannot* take my mother! There's so much I want to do for her and make up to her . . . she's suffered so much."

I got no further. The Lord spoke to me so clearly: *My son, what do you have to give to her, compared with what I have for her?*

That stopped me cold. "Lord . . . I don't have a thing . . . compared to what You have to give her. She's wanted to be with You for so long. Lord, You just go ahead and take her. She's Yours."

When I came out of the bathroom, Al spoke to me about getting a room. "No . . . I won't have to do that, Al," I replied calmly. *"The Lord is going to take her home."*

Al looked at me, startled, and reminded me that the doctors had said she could go on like this for weeks.

We went back to the hospital. I sat with Mother, realizing this would be the last time I would ever see her alive in this life. I told her how much I loved her. I read her favorite hymns and her favorite passages of Scripture, including Paul's glorious statement of faith in Romans 8:35–39 NIV:

> *Who shall separate us from the love of Christ? Shall trouble or hardship or persecution or famine or nakedness or danger or sword? As it is written:*
> *"For your sake we face death all day long;*
> *we are considered as sheep to be*
> *slaughtered."*
> *No, in all these things we are more than conquerors through him who loved us. For I am convinced that neither death nor life, neither angels nor demons, neither the present nor the future, nor any powers, neither height nor depth, nor anything else in all creation, will be able to separate us from the love of God that is in Christ Jesus our Lord.*

Mother was smiling and mumbling the words after me as I read. With my eyes filled with tears, I leaned into her oxygen tent and held her hands and gently kissed her forehead one last time. I prayed that God would take her home to be with Him. I zipped up her oxygen tent.

Then we left for dinner. We were at the restaurant only fifteen minutes when the hospital called to say that Mother had died. She had now graduated into the arms of her beautiful Savior, whom she had loved so much. She had fought the good fight; she had kept the faith. In her life, like Mary, the sister of Lazarus, she had loved to sit at Jesus' feet. Now she was in His bosom, safe forever. Suffering ended. Whole at last. *Hallelujah!* And I had His peace and joy as well.

What can I say about my mother's life? She had endured for sixteen years with tuberculosis. She had lost her husband; she had lost her health; for many years, she had lost her "wee lambs." But through all those years of suffering and loss, her faith in God and His love never wavered but instead increased. Her life was a testimony of Christian courage and faith.

How wonderful for her to hear the words, "Well done, good and faithful servant . . . enter into the joy of your Lord" (*see* Matthew 25:21).

When I was pleading with God for Mother's life—at best a few more pain-wracked years—hadn't He whispered in my heart: *What do you have for her, compared with what I have for her?*

What indeed. . . .

11. The Cellar

Therefore whatsoever ye have spoken in darkness shall be heard in the light; and that which ye have spoken in the ear in closets shall be proclaimed upon the housetops.

Luke 12:3 KJV

Mother's funeral was held in Dover, New Jersey. Auntie was there, as well as Uncle Norman and Aunt Louise and their children, and other relatives and friends. It was comforting to be with them again.

I shed many tears at the funeral, but they were tears of joy. There is a Scripture that embodies my attitude about my mother: "I consider that our present sufferings are not worth comparing with the glory that will be revealed in us" (Romans 8:18 NIV).

Back at Uncle Norman's house, friends and relatives gathered to share their memories of Mother and to console one another.

After everyone left, including Al, who was flying back west, Uncle Norman said, "Come down to the basement, Ike. There's something I want to tell you."

I thought maybe he wanted to discuss the funeral expenses. Mother had not been able to buy insurance because of her TB. Al paid for the entire funeral, so I had already decided I'd just have to stay out of school and work until I paid him back my share. That is, unless Uncle Norman were about to pull a rabbit out of a hat and tell me of some secret family fortune stashed somewhere.

I really loved and respected Uncle Norman; he had been the closest thing to a father to me. We had had long talks down in the basement many times before.

"Ike," he began, "I'm going to tell you something we promised your mother no one would ever tell you about until she was gone.

"Your Dad . . . uh, he . . . didn't die in a hunting accident, as you've been told. He actually committed suicide."

I was shocked. Dad . . . my hero . . . *a suicide?*

"He committed suicide?" I exclaimed. "My mother told me it was a hunting accident!" Talk about the old one-two punch: I was almost more stunned to think that my mother had told me a lie than that my father was a suicide! I just couldn't believe it. She was so committed to God—how could she have lied to me? And it was totally incomprehensible to me that my father could have shot himself, leaving my mother and us to fend for ourselves.

Then something clicked in the back of my mind. Yes . . . something Grandma Keay had said during my visit to Scotland in 1955, when she showed me the barn. . . . *and your father didn't kill himself, either.* At the time I thought it was a bizarre thing to say . . . but now, it all added up.

"Why in the world would my father have committed suicide?"

"Ike," he replied, "I'm not sure about all the details . . . but your dad had been running around with women for years. Your mother even came over here in 1935 with you boys for three months . . . to get away, because they were having problems."

My father, the man I had idolized as a boy . . . *a womanizer?* This had to be a nightmare . . . it couldn't be true!

I was more baffled than I was angry. Why had Mother let us go on all those years, thinking our father was a good man? I was remembering those letters from Mother about his being so strong and clean, when he really had been . . . *an adulterer!*

Uncle Norman explained that the reason Mother had lied was a totally honorable one: She knew we needed a strong, decent role model on which to pattern our lives. She knew the trauma of being separated from her was already almost too much for us. Had we known the terrible truth about our father's suicide on top of that . . . well, it probably would have destroyed us. We didn't need to know the whole truth at that time. We were too vulnerable.

And how wise Mother was to handle things as she did—to exact the promise from the family that we weren't to know the truth until we were grown. Mother knew that Al's character and mine would be formed by then, and we would be able to bear the truth, grim as it was. How brave she was, too, I thought, to have carried that awful secret in her heart all those years.

But Uncle Norman's story got much worse.

"Now . . . there was this girl," he continued. "She was fourteen, I think. She was coming up to the farm with her father to see your Dad. She was pregnant. And your dad just went out in the barn and killed himself . . . but I'm not really sure about the details. . . ."

It was horrible! Poor mother—what she must have suffered! Then it hit me like a blow: *My dad loved sex more than he did his family!*

At Bonnie Brae, I had prided myself on the fact that my father wasn't a drunk and a brute like some of the other boys' fathers. No . . . my dad was a clean-living athlete. It wasn't his fault we were at a home . . . he had died. And I cherished the idea that he had died a clean, honorable man. Now, to find it was all a sham. . . .

And it was maddening, not knowing all the facts. I had to know every sordid detail surrounding my father's death, but no one knew any more than what Uncle Norman had told me.

I was not to learn the full story until 1974, when I went back to Scotland with my family. My relatives were pretty tight-lipped about the details, so I looked up my mother's best friend, Aunt Margaret, who was by then in her eighties and in a nursing home. She told me the whole grim truth.

"Your father," Margaret began, "was having an affair with a fourteen-year-old girl who worked in his office. This girl used to come up to the house and play with you boys. She would tell you, 'How would you like to be my little boys? I'm going to marry your father and take you away. And I'll be your new mother.'

"And that would scare you, and you would say, 'No . . . you can't take us away from our mother!' And you would cry. And of course, your mother found out about it. Even I knew about it.

"In fact, your mother was packing to leave your father. She

was going to do it suddenly, without telling him. She was going to take you boys back to your Granda' Smith in the States, the very day it happened."

"Was the girl pregnant?" I asked. "Uncle Norman said she might have been."

"No . . . not at all," she replied. "Your Grandpa Keay caught them in bed together at her house. He had suspected for a long time that your dad was fooling around, and this day he decided to check on it.

"Anyway . . . he told your dad to get back up to the house and wait for him there. He was talking to this girl, trying to find out just how long the affair had been going on, when her father walked in.

" 'What are you doing in my house?' he asked.

"Well, it didn't take him long to figure out what was going on. The whole story came out. The man was in a rage. He told his daughter to get to her bedroom, that he'd deal with her later. Then he got on the phone and called the police.

"Now, the girl's in her room, listening to what they're saying, and when she hears her father call the police, she climbs out her window and runs up to the main house to warn your dad that the police are on the way to arrest him!

"When your dad heard that, he grabbed his shotgun and went out to the barn and shot himself in the head . . . to avoid the disgrace.

"You, Izat, were playing in the yard. Evidently you saw him go into the barn with the gun. You were only five at that time . . . just a wee thing. And you got up from your toys and began to follow him to the barn.

"You and your grandmother both heard the shot. She came running out the back door and got to the barn just as you had your hand on the doorknob to open it. She pulled you away and opened the door. She saw your dad lying there—with his head blown away, the shotgun beside him. It was a terrible, terrible sight for a mother to see.

"Your grandmother always said it's a good thing she got there before you did. No telling what effect seeing that would have had on you . . . you were such a wee laddie then.

"Well, as soon as your mother heard what had happened, she and I quickly unpacked her bags before the police arrived. We knew how it would look—she with her bags all packed and her husband lying dead in the barn. Oh . . . it was just a terrible, terrible thing.

"It was all hushed up. The papers listed the death as accidental. After all, he was dead. What would have been gained by dragging your family through the mud? Your cousins probably have the newspaper story somewhere. . . ."

I thanked Aunt Margaret for telling me the whole story. After twenty-seven years I finally knew the truth about my family: *The marriage was over. Mother was leaving him that very day.* As a little boy I never sensed anything was wrong between them. I loved them both. My dad had been a good father to me. He was my teacher; he was my friend; he was my idol. We always did things together.

But my dad really wasn't a good father. He was a self-centered man. He put his own personal desires before us, never considering what the consequences might be. We all paid a horrendous price for his sins.

I kept going back to Romans 8:28 (KJV): "And we know that all things work together for good to them that love God. . . ."

God was able to take even that terrible experience and give it meaning for my life. In a strange way—one I could never have foreseen—it was to result in great good for myself and others.

12. Carolyn

Who can find a virtuous woman? for her price is far above rubies. The heart of her husband doth safely trust in her, so that he shall have no need of spoil. She will do him good and not evil all the days of her life.

Proverbs 31:10–12 KJV

In the wake of the funeral and Uncle Norman's shocking disclosure, I was out of school for eight months while I worked to help pay back Al for half of Mother's funeral expenses.

I had previously learned the basics of carpentry, so now I was able to get a job in New Jersey.

At the Millington Baptist Church, I was more or less an assistant to the pastor. I worked with the youth group and young married couples.

People thought I was working too hard on the job and at church. Friends were always trying to fix me up with the single women at church. I wasn't interested. But they refused to give up. My friend Lois said to me, "Ike, you're twenty-six now. God is *not* going to put a girl in your lap! You've got to get out and start hunting."

I thanked her for her genuine concern but said, "Lois, if God wants me to marry, then He'll put a girl in my lap. I don't have to go out looking for one."

With strong encouragement from Pastor Harry Morris, I made last-minute plans and returned to Moody Bible Institute in January 1958. The pastor didn't know it, but I didn't even have the money for gasoline to drive to Chicago, let alone the other expenses. But I knew this was God's will and that He would supply everything.

At the Sunday-evening service, the night before I left, a

number of people came to me and gave me "love gifts." I had said nothing to anyone, yet now I was on my way—with sufficient money to get there!

Moody . . . oh, it was so good to be back! Almost immediately, I ran into my buddy Craig.

"Say, what did you and Carolyn do about your engagement?" I asked.

Somewhat wistfully, he replied, "Ike, we broke it off."

I was taken aback, even though I had questioned whether or not they were right for each other.

"It was for the best," Craig said. "It just wasn't working out . . . I guess it wasn't the Lord's will for either of us. I feel much better now, and Carolyn and I are still friends."

A few days later, I was walking down the hall to class when I ran into Carolyn.

"Ike! How are you?" she said, giving me a big smile. "It's really great to see you again! Everybody's been talking about your coming back. . . ." Then her pretty face clouded over. "Oh, Ike . . . I was so sorry to hear about your mother."

I thanked her for her condolences. It was just a short conversation, and then we parted. I couldn't help but notice that she didn't seem upset about the breakup with Craig.

But something more important had happened. On the surface it was just a chance meeting of two people who were casually acquainted. But the instant I laid eyes on Carolyn, God spoke very clearly to my heart:

This is the girl I have chosen for you to marry.

I knew it was the Lord because I had no intention of dating *any* girls. And although I had always considered Carolyn attractive, I never thought of her romantically at all. Not only had she been engaged to my friend but I had been too busy working and studying to even think about women. The advice I had offered the two of them had been sincerely given, with no ulterior motive.

Now, I suddenly thought Carolyn was *adorable* . . . her smile was *entrancing* . . . her hazel eyes were *captivating* . . . her every gesture was *vivacious*. . . . Yet, I was flabbergasted at the thought of Carolyn and me as anything more than friends.

Imagine her surprise when I began to pursue her aggressively. Every day I was asking her to lunch, to dinner, walking her to her dorm, taking her to concerts, church services, and other campus functions. The reason was simple: Having gotten the "green light" from the Lord, I saw no reason to waste any time. At age twenty-six I wasn't going to let any grass grow under my feet.

Carolyn was bowled over by my attentions, but after a series of romances that had soured for one reason or another, she was hesitant.

However, I was persistent. So, after only a few days of seeing me at her door every time she opened it, she began to soften. . . .

I was committed before I asked Carolyn out. She very clearly was God's choice for me. After only a few months of dating, I "unofficially" proposed to Carolyn in the Moody library.

I was studying homiletics—that's a fancy word for preaching. One night when we were studying, I pulled out a critique sheet containing guidelines for evaluating a preacher. I began filling in the blanks and telling Carolyn the answers: "Eye Contact: fantastic!; Body Language: superb!" When we got to the sermon, under the heading "Proposition," I wrote one and slid the paper over to her. It read, "I love you . . . will you marry me?"

She wrote a great big YES and returned it to me. We weren't officially engaged because I didn't have a ring to give her, but we were committed to each other.

Carolyn Conrad was born in St. Louis, Missouri, to a middle-class family. Some of her family background was similar to mine. She, too, had a younger brother (Jim). She also had a mother with a family history of tuberculosis. And she also had a father who had died young.

Carolyn's mother, Jane, had spent five years in a sanitarium, but by the time she was twenty, the TB was in remission. On a Christmas leave in 1932, she eloped and was married.

Carolyn's father, James Conrad, was a salesman for a sheet-metal company, as well as a professional singer. Carolyn was always close to her dad. She began to take piano lessons at five, and one of her girlhood dreams was to become so accomplished that she could accompany her father when he sang, as her mother sometimes did.

But in 1949, when Carolyn was twelve, her dream suddenly ended. Her father had a massive heart attack the day before Father's Day and died the day after—his beautiful voice stilled forever on earth at age forty-one.

It was a devastating blow to the family. Because he had been healthy and robust, Carolyn's dad had little insurance. Two weeks before he died he had turned down additional insurance because he felt he couldn't afford it. There was only two thousand dollars—just enough to pay for the funeral and burial, with very little left over.

As crushed as Carolyn and young Jim were by their father's death, their mother was devastated. She and Jim, Senior, hadn't merely been married; they were sweethearts. But this grief-stricken woman, left with two dependent children, rose to the challenge.

Shortly before Jim's death, Jane had begun to give demonstrations of Stanley Home Products to supplement the family income. Now, as the sole breadwinner, she threw herself into her sales work. Carolyn and Jim began going along to the Stanley parties to help their mother. Both children were happy to pitch in. Carolyn wanted to console her widowed mother and to help in any way she could.

For her part, Jane was determined to keep the family together at all costs. Realizing she had to increase her skills if she were ever going to earn a decent living, she set about teaching herself to type in her spare time, using a discarded typewriter and an old instruction book.

She became proficient enough that she was eventually hired as a secretary by the leading radiologist in St. Louis. Before long, she became an x-ray technician, in spite of the fact that she had never had the opportunity to finish high school!

As a very small child, Carolyn had accepted Christ as her Savior and was always telling neighborhood children about Jesus. She felt she had a calling to go into full-time Christian service.

At Moody, Carolyn studied Christian Education, with the idea of working with children on the mission field. But she eventually shifted her major to Bible.

Our entire courtship lasted seven months. Carolyn graduated in June 1958 and immediately left for Europe to tour with the Moody Chorale.

Once again I returned to Bonnie Brae as a relief housefather for three months. It was going to be a long, hot summer without Carolyn. But her letters, postmarked from all over the continent, helped. In one of them she wrote, "Ike, even though we're not formally engaged, sweetheart, I'm remaining true to you. . . ."

That made my heart do a flip-flop. We had promised we would write three letters a week, and they were coming like clockwork.

Then, for two or three weeks . . . nothing. I began to be concerned. Almost immediately I brought the Lord into it. "Lord," I prayed, "if Carolyn *is* the girl You've chosen for me, there is no way I can lose her." And God's perfect peace prevailed.

In one letter, Carolyn wistfully mentioned something about the other kids in the chorale who were engaged. Well, just about that time, I finally paid off having my mother's engagement ring put into a new setting for Carolyn. I couldn't wait for her to come home to give her a ring. Literally! Having prayed earnestly about it, I felt led to send her the ring—all the way to Europe.

From a commonsense perspective, mailing that ring was very risky. The Moody Chorale was traveling to a new city, a new country, every couple of days. I would have to catch her in just the right city on just the right day. Given the vagaries of the international mails, anyone would have said I was crazy to send that valuable diamond ring to her.

But this is where faith supersedes common sense. God was

my Mailman. As I posted the tiny box I prayed, *Lord, from my hand . . . to Your hand . . . to Carolyn's hand. Please get it safely to her.*

The chorale was singing in a small town in Sweden when the ring caught up with Carolyn. She was notified that a small package was at the local post office. But she couldn't get it out. There was red tape that would take days to straighten out, plus a whopping import duty to be paid on the diamond. And Carolyn didn't have the money. To make matters worse, the chorale was leaving early that very day.

So they all went down to the post office. The tour leader went to bat for Carolyn, pleading with officials to bend the rules a little.

In God's providence, a woman postmistress happened to be on duty that day . . . she listened sympathetically to a tale of separated sweethearts and an heirloom ring that had been sent in faith thousands of miles across continents and seas.

After some anxious moments of deliberation, the postmistress handed Carolyn the little box, which was all crushed and splayed open. (The real miracle was that the ring was still inside!)

As Carolyn slipped the beautiful ring on her finger, her girlfriends crowded around, squealing with delight. Even the postmistress was beaming as she waived the import duty. Everybody agreed it was the most romantic engagement ever.

You can imagine my delight when I finally received a long-awaited answer to my proposal in the form of a short cablegram from my sweetheart: "Yes! '. . . where you go, I will go, and where you lodge, I will lodge. Your people shall be my people, and your God, my God' " (Ruth 1:16 NAS).

So, there was Carolyn—in Sweden. And there was I—in New Jersey. We were four thousand miles apart. But we were finally, officially engaged! *And we were one in the Lord. . . .*

13. The Two Shall Become One

. . . for this cause a man shall leave his father and mother, and shall cleave to his wife; and the two shall become one flesh.

Matt. 19:5 NAS

Carolyn's boat docked in New York in mid-August. It was wonderful to see her again. She looked absolutely beautiful. But we were somehow different with each other: Now we were officially engaged to be married—promised to one another in the sight of man and of God.

She stayed in New Jersey for the remaining two weeks of my summer contract with Bonnie Brae Farm. During that time, we decided to get married right away, in September. Carolyn dreaded telling her mother because even though we wanted only a simple ceremony and reception, four weeks was hardly time enough to prepare for a wedding.

In late August, we drove back to St. Louis and called Carolyn's minister, Dr. J. Allen Blair. He came over and talked to us. When he saw that in spite of the short notice we had looked for God's counsel and were not entering into our marriage plans lightly, he gave us his blessing.

Carolyn, of course, had just graduated from Moody. I had two years to go. But when I wrote to inform the school that we were going to be married, I received the answer that if we did, I couldn't come back for one year—it was the rule. At the rate I was going, I wondered if I would ever finish school, but we felt it was the Lord's timing. Both of my parents were now gone, and for a year I had had no real home. Besides, I wasn't getting any younger. I was nearly twenty-seven; Carolyn was twenty-two. I didn't want to be an old father to my teenage children.

We were married at Carolyn's home in a simple ceremony on September 12, 1958, with only family and close friends in attendance. You can be sure that when I took my marriage vows it was a very serious occasion for me, in light of my father's failure.

Finally, my life seemed complete: After all the sorrow of my childhood, God was graciously giving me a wonderful wife. We were starting our marriage as a Christian couple. A verse of Scripture that was very meaningful to us was, "O magnify the Lord with me, and let us exalt his name together" (Psalms 34:3 KJV). This was the prayer of our hearts as we entered a most important chapter of our lives. I had waited patiently for the Lord, and He had chosen the right woman for me—a helpmate who was far better and lovelier than anyone I could have imagined.

After a weekend honeymoon in the Ozarks, Carolyn and I returned to her mother's home in St. Louis. I immediately went to work for a Christian carpenter from Carolyn's church. Carolyn got a job at the St. Louis County Bank.

Within three days trouble struck. Mom Conrad began coughing up blood and was rushed to the hospital. Her illness was directly related to her girlhood bout with TB.

Mom was gravely ill and had to have one of her lungs removed. I grieved for her suffering, having seen my own mother become an invalid because of the disease.

Carolyn's mother's illness brought Carolyn and me even closer together. We spent the first three weeks of our marriage working all day and running back and forth to the hospital nights and weekends. Then, after Mom's release, she was convalescing at home for another three months. Carolyn and I pitched in with the chores and helped care for our patient until she got back on her feet.

Eventually Mom recovered. Once she was up and around and back at work, and after seeking the Lord's will in the matter, Carolyn and I decided it was time to strike out on our own. Carolyn's brother, Jim, was living at home and going to Covenant College, and he could look out for his mom.

In June 1959 we took another job, right in St. Louis, so we could be near Mom. It was a live-in position at the Evangelical Children's Home, a million-dollar facility.

It seemed an ideal situation; we would be out on our own and working in child care (a ministry to which I felt the Lord was calling me). We had our own small apartment: one bedroom and a bath in a cottage with twelve to fourteen rowdy boys!

We weren't going to be alone for long in our little love nest at the home. A few months before we took the job, we had learned that Carolyn was expecting a baby! So by the time we actually made the move, Carolyn was well along in her pregnancy.

I could hardly believe it: *me,* a father! I felt ten feet tall. If only Mother could have lived to see our baby.

Our beautiful little girl was born on September 12, 1959, exactly one year after our marriage. Our darling baby was the greatest anniversary gift any couple ever gave each other. We named her Kimberly Ann Keay—Ann because my mother, Johanna, was called Anna.

She was a little beauty with strawberry blonde hair, dark, sparkling eyes, and cute cheeks, just like her mom.

When Carolyn and I took the job at the Evangelical Children's Home, we had both been looking forward to the challenge of nurturing children and introducing them to the Lord—the very thing Bonnie Brae had stopped me from doing. We felt it was our calling, as surely as if we had been missionaries to India or Japan. And of course, we had been looking for independence and the privacy so important to young marrieds.

It quickly became apparent, however, that we had gone from the frying pan into the fire!

At the children's home, we were on call literally twenty-four hours a day, taking care of those fourteen active boys, six of whom were emotionally disturbed delinquents.

Adding to our problems, Baby Kim had a terrible case of colic and kept us awake all night, nearly every night, for three or four months. There was no end to it; she cried day and night. And the three of us were in one small bedroom! It would have been a tough enough situation for any new parents, but on top of that, we had all those boys to care for.

And since I was going to school at Midwest Bible College full-time, poor Carolyn was left holding the bag.

The boys in our cottage were captivated by little Kim. They were forever wanting to see her, touch her, hold her, and entertain her. Being around a baby was good for the boys, no doubt, and we didn't want to deny them. But privately, Carolyn complained that she wanted our baby to herself, not on public display. Carolyn and I had almost no time alone with our baby or, for that matter, with each other.

"Honey, I'm afraid I'm not as giving as you," she said with a bit of a pout. "Let's face it: I'm selfish! I want you and my baby to myself. Is that too much to ask for?"

I had to sympathize with Carolyn. The situation was particularly stressful on her because not only was she a new young wife wanting to be alone with her husband and baby but also she had been raised in a normal, quiet family environment. I had lived at a boys' home all those years and was used to the constant bustle and noise of rowdy boys coming and going, laughing and fighting, working and playing. Carolyn was totally unprepared for the constant demands of institutional life.

The situation was aggravated for her by lack of sleep. Because I had to be alert for school in the morning, I took to sleeping in the boys' quarters, so I wasn't affected by Kim's incessant crying all through the night.

Night after night, Carolyn walked the floor, with Kim screaming in her ear. Then she had to get up and put in a full day with fourteen active boys.

There was only one solution: I dropped out of school again. It helped somewhat; at least I took those boys off Carolyn's hands. But things were still too much. She began to crack under the strain. So great was the stress and lack of sleep that she actually began to talk about committing suicide.

The upshot was that we had to quit our job after only nine months at the home. We quickly packed and moved closer to the college. It was a disappointment, to be sure, but Carolyn's health had to come first.

It was February 1959. The building trades had practically closed down for the winter, so I couldn't get work as a carpenter anywhere. In desperation, I took a job as a salesman, trudging door-to-door in the bitter cold, selling pots and pans. I supplemented this with any work I could get through a temp agency. Things got really bad—*nobody* wanted pots. So I stayed home for a while with the baby, and Carolyn took a temporary job.

In the spring of 1959, we moved to a large subdivision in St. Louis. I got a break when the owner began work on a new subdivision. He gave me a good job laying out the apartments in the new subdivision. (I had attended night school and had become a journeyman carpenter, so I caught on quickly.)

The exciting news during this time of testing was that Carolyn and I were expecting our second child. Little Deborah, our cute little blonde with the biggest blue eyes you ever saw, was born on October 11, 1960, just thirteen months after Kim.

With two babies and a wife to provide for, I was thankful for that construction job. Still, Carolyn and I realized it was stopgap. We both knew we had a higher calling, to be in some kind of Christian service. We were just waiting on the Lord.

An old friend was visiting and told us of a Christian home in North Carolina. "It's a children's home that desperately needs a man to do maintenance and also to work with the children," he said. "That's right up your alley, Ike."

"Where is it?" I asked.

"Well, it's in the boondocks—in fact, Appalachia. A place called Bitter Creek. Gosh, it's nothing fancy, like your last home. And it's real mountain country, with mountain people—a mission field with a great deal of poverty. The need is so great . . . why don't you consider it?"

"Oh, honey, let's look into it, at least!" Carolyn said.

Well, we did look into it. We wrote a letter to the director of the home. He then called me and we talked awhile. Walter Jones had a kind voice and spoke freely about his love for the Lord and for the children. He said he was very interested in hiring me. He liked the fact that I, too, had grown up in a children's home and was a committed Christian.

He said they needed some renovations done. I told him that would be no problem for me as a journeyman carpenter. Jones then told me it was my decision—provided, of course, we could raise our own support.

In effect, he was telling me the job was mine. That made me feel terrific. I thanked him and said we'd pray about his offer and also about the necessary support.

We never visited the Mountain Haven Children's Home beforehand, but Walter Jones did send us slides. It wasn't nearly as impressive as the million-dollar campus of the Evangelical Children's Home, but it was imposing. The main building was like a large Southern mansion, set high upon a hill. In the slides, the surrounding country appeared to have a wild sort of beauty.

Carolyn and I felt led to accept the offer. It would be such a challenge, and it was a way to work in home missions. From the slides, the children there seemed really appealing.

As soon as our church, Brentwood Bible, heard about our plans and our need for financial assistance, the members wanted to support us. Since the church was just three or four years old, Carolyn and I would be the very first missionary couple to be sent out. We were also given support by the Millington Baptist Church. Everyone was involved and excited about this new door the Lord had suddenly opened for us.

I had already given notice at work. Then one morning when I got to the construction site, I found that the foreman and all sixty-four carpenters had been fired—everyone except the boss's nephew and me. The boss wanted me to take over as foreman, with a big increase in pay!

I knew Satan was up to his old tricks again. He was dangling that big promotion and the money as bait, to keep me from going to that children's home. I figured that for some reason old Lucifer didn't want me going down there, where I was needed. I turned down that offer.

To think, we were actually going to be missionaries, right here in a needy area of the United States! It was the start of our dream come true!

Looking forward to that new, exciting experience of joyful service for the Lord, we had no way of knowing our "dream come true" would end in a dreadful nightmare. . . .

Radiant bride: Johanna and Izat Keay on their wedding day (June 5, 1926).

Left: Izat, junior, and his mother.

Above: Proud father and sons. Ike is on the left.

Left: Passport photo after Ike's father's death in 1937.

Right: Happy family a few weeks before the separation, 1941.

Below: Down on the farm (left to right): a friend, Ike, and Al, early 1940s.

Bottom Left: Johanna Keay spent almost ten years in a sanitarium.

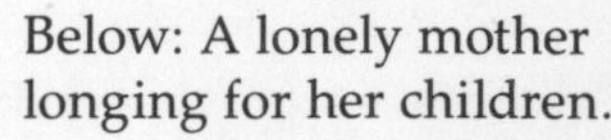

Below: A lonely mother longing for her children.

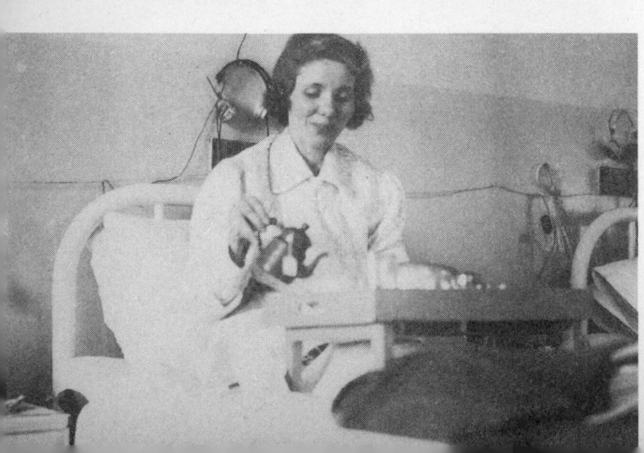

Above: Al and Ike enjoy a rare happy visit from their mother at Bonnie Brae, 1945.

Right: Coauthor William Deerfield (left) and Ike at Bonnie Brae, 1948.

Below: The Bonnie Brae baseball team, 1948. Al is in front, second from right. Ike is in the back row, third from right.

Right: Auntie Lizzie (left), Ike, and his mother while Ike was a houseparent at Bonnie Brae, 1956.

Above: Ike (left), scoutmaster and Eagle Scout, with his brother, Lieutenant Alexander Keay, U.S. Air Force, 1956.

Right: The closest thing to a father. Uncle Norman Smith (center), his son Norman, and Ike, 1956.

Prologue: Carolyn and Ike with daughters Kim (left) and Debbie, moments before Deb's near drowning and miraculous rescue, 1962.

Where it all began in 1954. The Hassler House of what was then Bethel Bible School.

Inset: Prison evangelist and founder of Bethel, the Reverend Floyd Hipp (1897-1970).

Right: Board Christmas Banquet, 1986. Seated are founder's daughter, Mrs. Eleonore Williams (left), and founder's wife, Mrs. Helen Hipp. Standing are some of Bethel's children and charter board member and president Ted DeMoss.

Photo by Robin Rudd/courtesy of the *Chattanooga News-Free Press*.

Above: Scene from Bethel film *Crime's Forgotten Children*. This little girl just saw her father murder her mother.

Left: Four of Bethel's cherubs. "Red and yellow, black and white, they are precious in His sight."

Above: Entrance to Bethel Bible Village. Motto: Preventing crime by presenting Christ.
Right: Carolyn's stepfather and her mother, the Reverend George and Jane Stratton.
Below: Carolyn's brother and family, the Reverend Jim and Evie Conrad and children (left to right) Johnny, Andrew, and Laurie.

Left: Ike's brother, Alex, and his wife, Loralee.

Below: The Keay clan at son Brian's wedding, 1987. Front row (left to right): Brian, Carolyn, Alan. Back row (left to right): new daughter-in-law, Anne, Debbie, Ike, Kim and husband, Ali.

Right: The happy couple. Carolyn and Ike on twenty-fifth wedding anniversary, 1983.

Part Three

"Suffer the Little Children. . . ."

Questions and Answers

"Where is Jesus when you need Him?
They've abused a little child!"
We said we didn't want Him;
He was too meek and mild.

"Where is Jesus when you need Him?
There are little children crying!"
He's hanging where we nailed Him,
And He's very busy dying.

"Where is Jesus when you need Him?
He'll never come again!"
When you help the hurting children,
Christ will have saved them . . . then.

WILLIAM DEERFIELD

14. The Lions' Den

My God hath sent his angel, and hath shut the lions' mouths, that they have not hurt me. . . .

Daniel 6:22 KJV

Let me say at the outset that the Mountain Haven Children's Home was not the real name of that facility toward which we were so hopefully headed in June 1962. And it was not in Bitter Creek; there is no such place in North Carolina. The home, in fact, was not even in that state. To protect the privacy of persons involved, we have changed names and locales.

We arrived at the place after dark, in a raging thunderstorm. The rain was coming down in sheets, rendering the windshield wipers practically useless—pretty nerve-racking when you are driving through the mountains in strange country after dark. But the Lord was with us, and we got there without mishap. As previously arranged, we rendezvoused at a little Baptist Church in Bitter Creek with a staff member from the home, George Stratton, who was going to take us up to the home. He didn't want us to get lost in the dark.

"How are you folks tonight?" Stratton asked, smiling and extending his hand and giving me a firm shake.

George Stratton was a tall, rangy man with handsome, craggy features, who gave off what the kids nowadays call "good vibes." He suggested we leave our car and transfer to the home's carryall, rugged jeeplike vehicle that could hold ten people or so. It had a bulldog gear (double-low) to negotiate the steep, rugged terrain. As soon as we started up the mountain in that rainstorm, we knew why they needed a vehicle like that.

The road—if you could call it that—was deeply rutted and covered with rocks. That grade was so steep, the headlights were hardly hitting the road. They were shining up into a stormy sky, through which lightning zigzagged. Our car would never have made it.

At the top of the hill, through the driving rain, we saw the main building, illumined by flashes that split the darkness. It rose proud and imposing above us and had what had to be (in clear weather) a commanding view of the valley below. There were a number of smaller buildings, including one that Stratton pointed out as the school.

He drove us not to the main building but to a little trailer and unloaded us. This—as we understood it—was to be our temporary home, until I could renovate the former director's home, which Mr. Jones had told me would be ours.

I must say that old trailer was pretty small—only about eight feet by twenty-four—particularly for two adults and two children.

George Stratton apologized for the accommodations. He said he didn't live on campus. Once he carried the last suitcase in, he told us that the director, Walter Jones, would take us up to breakfast in the morning. Then he politely bade us good night.

That first night, all night long, there was howling somewhere out in the rain-swept darkness. Lightning flashed around that mountain and thunder boomed. Carolyn scrunched up to me in the darkness. "Oh, honey, that sounds like . . . *wolves!*" she whispered.

"It's only stray dogs," I replied, not at all sure. "Let's try to get some sleep."

In the morning the sun was shining. Walter Jones came down to get us. He asked if we had passed a good night, in spite of the rain and thunder.

He was about forty, with thinning hair. He was very pleasant and warm, almost sweet; it was obvious he was eager to make us feel welcome.

In the morning sun, the home looked beautiful. We all walked up to the dining hall, which was in the main building. It was a regular mansion with, I figured, probably twenty to twenty-five large rooms. It was covered with white clapboard and had a wide, handsome veranda.

The dining hall wasn't very big; it was about half the size of the one at Bonnie Brae. There were about forty to fifty kids seated at tables with adults when we walked in.

Walter took us around and introduced us to the various staff members. Of course, the children were excited. They looked like a nice group of kids; the boys had their hair slicked down and the girls were all in pigtails and little neatly starched dresses.

Walter then took us to the main table, where he introduced us to the founders of the home, Mr. Richard Claxton and his wife, Betty ("Mom" and "Pop" to the kids). Pop was a short, rather stout balding man of about seventy, with strong features and glasses. He seemed to be a very friendly, kind man. His wife was a warm, matronly woman. We were also introduced to Walter's wife, Margaret, who was the founders' daughter—which made Pop Claxton Walter's father-in-law.

We had a pleasant breakfast; the food was plain but good. "We're sure glad the Lord brought you folks here," Pop said. "Of course, it goes without saying that Mountain Haven is a Christian home. We're strict, Bible-believing people here. I know from Walter that you folks are, too," he added with a quick smile. "Our children are well-behaved. We believe in 'spare the rod and spoil the child,' as the Bible says. But we do surely love these little ones. I guess Walter told you they come from very poor families or broken homes."

"Yes, he did," I replied.

'I founded this home about fifteen years ago," Pop Claxton continued. "We're pretty proud of it. Glad to have you with us."

The Claxtons were a godly couple, I quickly decided. Sweet and warm, too—and the hardest-working people I'd ever seen. They adored the children.

Although Pop and Mom delegated the day-to-day management of Mountain Haven Home to their son-in-law, they were the ones with the clout; they ultimately set the policies. And they ran a tight ship.

The first few months, I didn't have a great deal of contact with the kids, which was disappointing. But after all, I had been hired to do maintenance. I spent my days renovating two houses, one of which we were to move into.

I was anxious to get that place livable because Carolyn was having problems with that cramped trailer. We weren't there a month when the little gas range blew up in her face, singeing her hair and eyebrows. And the water turned her laundry brown. (Laundry blueing turned things green.) Then in July, the water gave out and we had to haul it in buckets.

It was wild country there. The animal life consisted of foxes, scorpions, copperheads, and rattlers. After we got moved into the house, one of the staff members killed a copperhead just off the front porch, where Kim and Debbie played.

After a while, Carolyn and I noticed the Claxtons played favorites. There were very pretty little twin sisters, about ten years old, who got all sorts of favors from both Mom and Pop. We knew it wasn't fair, and the other kids resented it, too.

But the Claxtons were devout. Every night after dinner, Pop would sit in one of the big living rooms, reading aloud from the Bible. It wasn't like evening devotions; he would be reading but not to anyone in particular. Kids and staff members would be coming and going, doing their own thing, and Pop would be reading away, sometimes his voice falling into a mumble, as if he were reading to himself.

In late August, Walter called me to his office and told me a teacher was needed to handle seventh and eighth grades. Would I be interested? I jumped at it. Here was my chance to be with the children, to interact with them and give them the guidance they needed.

I soon discovered I was a natural-born teacher. And since I had had a tough time as a schoolboy, I could sympathize with the kids when they couldn't understand things. They related to me, particularly when they learned I had grown up in a children's home, just like them.

It was about the time I began teaching that I noticed a change in the Claxtons' attitude toward me. It wasn't obvious; on the contrary, it was so subtle that at first I thought I was imagining it—an imperceptible cooling of their usual warmth.

Then, after comparing notes with George Stratton and some of the other staff, it hit me: They were jealous of the fact that the children liked me and came to me with their problems. I was invading their turf!

It was a startling conclusion, but I could almost understand why they were jealous. They loved those children so much. They had worked so hard through the years, and these were "their" children. We were the new kids on the block.

But there was more to it. As the weeks passed it became more and more obvious that Mom and Pop wanted the staff to do their work and leave the children to them. Maybe that's why there had been such a tremendous staff turnover. I was told that in the previous two years about twenty people had come and gone.

Pop lavished attention on those little girls. He would even feed some of them, like a doting father, or let them eat off his plate. He wasn't the same with the boys.

One day I was walking across the campus when I saw him switching one of the boys on the legs. He was holding the child, who couldn't have been more than ten, by the hand, and flailing away.

Whish! Whish! Whish! Again and again the switch descended on the boy's bare legs.

The boy was pulling away, attempting to avoid the sting of the switch, causing the two of them to move in a circle as if they were engaged in some kind of bizarre dance. The child's face was a mask of pain but he never uttered a sound. After hitting him about ten times, Pop sat down to rest, but in a few seconds he was up again, beating him some more.

It wasn't just the switching that shocked me; it was the expression on Pop's face: I saw fierce anger in his eyes. I thought, *You can discipline a child in love. But this discipline is not in love. . . .*

One day after class, I was getting my books together when

two girls came up to my desk and said, "Mr. Keay . . . Pop says he saw you peeping in our window."

"Oh, is that so?" I replied, barely looking at them. I knew the tricks kids can pull in children's homes, to set adult staff members against one another. He might switch the boys, but Pop was still a godly man. I could not imagine him saying such a mean, nasty thing.

But a few days later, one of the girls lingered after class again and in an almost fearful voice said, "Mr. Keay . . . last night Pop said right in front of some of the other kids that he saw you in the dark basement with a few girls. . . ."

"Sissy, you know that's not true," I said, looking up from my papers. "And furthermore, I can't picture Pop saying that. Now, come on. . . ."

"I know it ain't true. But he *did* say it."

There was genuine concern on Sissy's face. Something told me she wasn't making this up. But if she weren't . . . well, it was just too baffling.

A few days later Sissy was back with a couple of her friends. Now they were saying that Pop was telling the kids I had some of the girls down in the basement, only this time he said I was taking their panties down!

"Now . . . really, girls!" I said, mortified. "Is Pop really saying things like this? I can't believe it."

They stood there looking at one another, but no one spoke. "You girls wouldn't be making this up, would you . . . to make trouble between Pop and me?"

"Oh, no, Mr. Keay!" one of them protested. "He *is* saying it! Honest! He even said he saw you peeking in our bedroom windows at night, watching us get undressed."

"Yeah," one of the others chimed in, "he's sayin' this stuff about *you*, but *he's* been doin' stuff like that to us!"

I looked at her, trying to conceal my shock. The girl who said this was Sarah Ann Jordan. Sarah, who was about twelve, was at Mountain Haven with her younger sister, Cora Lee, and her brother Sammy. They were the second generation of the Jordan family to be at the home; older, grown sisters and brothers were now married.

Sarah was a real terror at the home. She was always into trouble of one kind or another and usually got away with murder. Mom and Pop Claxton, along with everyone else, had given up trying to correct her. She was a big problem in my classroom. One day she pushed her entire desk over and just sat there, glaring at me.

"Yeah, she does that and gets away with it!" sneered her brother. "Old Sarah gets away with everything! If *we* do it, we get it good!"

I had learned long ago that you can't have double standards with children, nor can you play favorites, so I said, "Well, she's not going to be treated special in my class; you'll all abide by the same rules."

I took her out of class and we talked about her behavior. Then I proceeded to give her the required discipline: switching on her bare legs. But after I had given her about four strokes, I broke down and cried. I had never hit a girl in my life. But this was standard procedure in the mountains.

I suspect that, seeing my tears, she realized how much I really did care.

Now Sarah was up to her old tricks again. *Or was she?* I went to one of our coworkers and told her what Sarah said. "Oh, Ike," she replied, "you know how that girl lies! Why, you can't believe what she says."

A few days later Sarah told me that when the children were being driven over to church to a Youth for Christ meeting, the boys were reaching around the seats and trying to put their hands up her skirt. Knowing boys, I wouldn't put it past them. But Sarah *was* given to telling wild stories. . . .

"But please don't say anything about it to anybody, Mr. Keay," she said, in earnest. "I don't want any trouble."

All of a sudden it hit me. This girl was not making things up. She was confiding in me, like Sissy. And if the story about the boys was true, what was I to make of her wild stories about Pop Claxton?

It was too terrible to contemplate, but I began to put things together. Why was it the Claxtons didn't want us to have much interaction with the children? I knew they were possessive of them, but could there be any other, perhaps more sinister, reason?

A short time later, I was talking to Mom Claxton about Sarah Ann's behavior problems when she suddenly said, "And Pop would never do anything wrong to these girls."

That struck a chord: Grandma Keay's sudden outburst during my 1955 visit to Scotland: "And your father didn't kill himself, either!"

Nobody had said my father killed himself. *But he had.* And nobody had said Pop was doing wrong to the girls.

Christmas came and went. Carolyn's mother visited and went to church with us a few times. George Stratton would make a beeline for us, a little quicker than usual, whenever Mom was with us. She was an attractive woman and a real lady. Carolyn and I began wondering if maybe there was a little romance in the air. . . .

The children were still telling me things, and the stories were getting worse and worse. The allegations came out in little bits and pieces. Paradoxically, the children loved Pop Claxton and had great loyalty toward him. But there must have been anger, too, for them to say such things. And the children had learned to love me also, so perhaps when Pop said bad things about me, they became angry with him.

Finally, one of the girls blurted out, "Yeah . . . after we go to bed at night, Pop comes in and tells us to come and get into his bed. And he does stuff to us. . . ."

By now I had heard too much, from too many of the kids. Even Sammy Jordan, Sarah's brother, told me, "If we get caught peeping in the girls' windows we get the switch. But then Pop turns around and does it his own self!"

I could get fired if I went to the director with allegations that couldn't be proved, and after all, Claxton was his father-in-law. I was in an agony of indecision.

In February, one of the home's board members was visiting. At one point he came to me and said, very pointedly, "There's sin in this home, and we're going to get to the bottom of it. We don't like that kind of thing!"

I thought, *Great! I hope they do get to the bottom of it.*

One visiting day, one of the alumnae of the home, a woman, approached me. "Mr. Keay . . . I've got to talk to you. Sarah says I can trust you, and I think I can." We went outside.

"What is it?" I said.

"Sarah told me she's been talking with you about Pop and the girls."

"Yes, she has," I answered, "but it's hard for me to believe that what she says is true."

"Mr. Keay, I *know* she's telling the truth!" she whispered. "I know, because Pop fooled around with me, when I was a girl here, too!"

I stared at her, mortified. The implications hit me like a ton of bricks. *He's been abusing these children for years.* My face must have revealed the shock. She moved in closer. "And I'll tell you somethin' else . . . I heard that he used to fool around with some of our mothers, too." All the pieces began falling in place, like some demonic jigsaw puzzle.

I went to talk to Walter Jones. Believe me, it was tough to tell him his father-in-law was a child molester! At first he didn't believe me. How could he?

"Walter, I know it's terrible, hearing something like this about your own father-in-law," I said. "I don't want to hurt your wife . . . say such things about her dad . . . I didn't believe it at first. I put off coming to you for as long as I could. But I've been hearing too many things from too many people. There has to be something to it!"

There was a long silence. "Walter . . . what can we do about this?"

Walter Jones was a good man but an indecisive one. He said he'd have to think about it.

* * *

That spring something else happened that didn't seem connected to the business with the founder.

There were two part-time maintenance men who shared a cabin in one of the nearby hollows.

Sarah and Cora Lee came to me one day with another story. "Mr. Keay, my brother Sammy says that those maintenance men are asking the boys if they can get some of us girls to meet them out in the woods."

After questioning the girls closely, it turned out that only one of the men, T. J., was actually involved; the other man, Horace, never said anything that was out of line. I believed the girls because I had chatted with Horace and knew he was a born-again Christian. He had a nice, decent way about him. But his buddy T. J. was the silent type, full of secrets.

I went to Walter with my new information. He hadn't yet acted on the allegations against his father-in-law, but he was now leaning toward believing the whole sordid story. After hearing about this latest mess he said, "You say Horace is not involved?"

"No . . . the kids say not."

"Then he can stay. I'll just lay off the other one since it's the end of the job."

As far as that mountain man knew, no other staff members were involved in his dismissal. Then Carolyn made a mistake.

She was teaching piano, and she happened to be talking to one of the boys about the allegations. The boy put two and two together and told T. J. it was me who had blown the whistle on him.

The next thing I knew, Walter called me to his office and said, "Ike . . . I don't know how to tell you this, but I'm hearing talk that T. J.'s saying the next time he catches you or your family off the mountain he's going to kill you. He's an angry man who is capable of anything! You and Carolyn spoke up. You are outsiders. These people are very clannish. It's not a question of right and wrong. . . ."

"Well, it is to me," I replied.

"All they know is you are outsiders sticking your noses in

where they shouldn't be . . . I don't want to alarm you, but I've heard he's shot at people.

"Ike," Walter concluded, "I would not make any trips into town right now, if I were you. And I'd keep my doors and windows locked."

I really appreciated Walter's concern, but I was sure I had done the right thing. The next few days, I'd walk out of our little house and I'd look up into the night sky, studded with stars, so vast in number, so eternal. And I'd think, *Lord, if You can make all those stars from nothing and put all of them up there, then it's a very small matter for You to take care of me and my family. If You want me in heaven, he's going to get me. But if You don't want me in heaven yet, there's no way he can get me! So I don't have to worry about it; I'm Your responsibility.*

So I didn't lock my door. I slept with my windows open at night. And I had absolute peace.

Carolyn was having a lot more trouble experiencing God's peace.

"Honey," I said, "the man is blind in one eye, anyway. Maybe he's a bad shot. . . ."

"Don't joke about it!" she cried. "Oh . . . it's all my fault! Me and my big mouth! Honey, will you forgive me?"

"There's nothing to forgive," I replied. "You were concerned and you talked about it."

I have always made it a practice to turn to God's Word during times of testing and meditate upon it and encourage my heart in the Lord, as David did in 1 Samuel 30:6.

So it was that during this time of testing I had put about ten or fifteen Bible verses in large lettering all over our kitchen cabinets. This was a great encouragement to us. When a man is gunning for your family, you'd better have something to hold on to, and hold on we did: "So do not fear, for I am with you; do not be dismayed, for I am your God. I will strengthen you and help you; I will uphold you with my righteous right hand" (Isaiah 41:10 NIV); " 'Do not be afraid or discouraged because of this vast army. For the battle is not yours, but God's' " (2

Chronicles 20:15 NIV). These and many other verses were our "spiritual vitamins" during this difficult time.

Finally, I told Carolyn I had made up my mind to go over and have it out with T. J. She begged me not to go. We had two little ones to think of. I told her the Lord was looking out for us and I had to go. But she was absolutely terrified.

Six days in a row I started to go over to T. J.'s cabin in the next hollow. T. J.'s buddy Horace warned me off each time. "Ike," he said, "T. J. is so mad, don't you even come *near* our place! Hear?" But I had to get it settled.

Early Sunday morning I said to Carolyn, "I'm going over. . . ." By that time she knew it was no use arguing. She just hugged me tight and let me go.

I drove the Jeep as far as I could into the hollow and then got out and started to walk the rest of the way. I knew there was no way to sneak up on the cabin because they had six or eight dogs.

I got to the end of the trail and saw the place. It was just a little two-room cabin, with a pile of new lumber and windows stacked neatly beside one wall, as if they were adding a room. The dogs started howling and barking when they heard the Jeep.

I had to walk the last hundred yards through the woods to get to the cabin. T. J. might be watching me from the window. He could easily take a bead on me. . . .

I started toward the cabin. "Lord," I prayed, "it's sure nice to have You here with me."

I walked up the sagging steps and knocked on the door. Pretty soon T. J. came out. He was a big, slow-moving man, but his eyes snapped with anger when he saw me. If looks could kill, I'd have been dead.

"T. J., I'd like to talk to you. We've got some things to settle." I said it as calmly as if I were discussing the weather, wondering all the while if he would snatch up his rifle and blast me away. Instead, he grunted and ambled out to the well, his dogs trotting beside him. He leaned his arm against the well upright and stared at the pile of lumber, as if waiting to hear what I had to say.

"Look, T. J.," I said, coming right to the point, "those kids told me what you had in mind." His head spun around and he shot me a glittery look with his good eye, as if warning me not to elaborate.

"I believe what they said is true. And you know it's true, too."

"I don't know no such thing!" he protested, kicking the dust.

My heart was racing. "As far as I'm concerned, you're guilty. You intended to fool around with those girls and you got fired for it. They're just young kids! In your heart you know you're guilty, and you got what was coming to you!"

There was a long silence while he glared off into space. Then, looking at me with a smile that really shocked me, he answered, "Now . . . look here, Ike, them kids is liars! And they know all about sex, too. They could teach a grown man some tricks! You know that . . . look, I don't want no trouble. Why don't we just forget the whole thing. I was mad, but I ain't got no hard feelin's no more."

I was startled. He had been threatening to kill my whole family, and now he wanted to forget the whole thing.

Maybe I was pressing things, but I said, "I have to tell you . . . I don't like my family being threatened!"

"I never threatened nobody . . . and whoever says I did is a cotton-pickin' liar! An' I'll tell 'em to their face!"

I was thankful he was only murdering the truth and not going for his rifle.

Having made my point, a few minutes later I started walking back across the clearing, thanking God for the change in T. J.'s attitude, but at the same time wondering if he were going to put a bullet in my back as I returned to my Jeep. Rejoicing in God's protection, I slid behind the wheel and drove off.

What a way to start the Lord's Day! Praise His Holy Name! A weight had been lifted from my shoulders.

Carolyn and all the others who had been praying during my absence were thrilled. God had given us the victory!

About a week or two later I received an official-looking letter from an attorney. It began:

> Mr. Keay:
>
> This letter is to inform you that criminal charges are being filed against you. Two witnesses have claimed. . . .

I was shocked. *T. J. had turned the tables: He and Horace were accusing me!*

According to the letter, they both swore they had seen me through a window at the school, having sexual relations with one of the girls from the home! No wonder T. J. had been so nice to me that day! He had decided on a different plan of attack. He was going to get me one way or another.

Heartsick, I read on:

> . . . I advise you to secure legal representation, as an indictment on criminal charges will undoubtedly be forthcoming. . . .

The letter concluded by hinting broadly that the only way I could avoid criminal prosecution would be to leave the area as soon as possible. Carolyn was devastated.

"Oh, honey, I hoped it was all over," she said. "I just knew something else was going to happen!"

I showed the letter to Walter and he suggested I see a lawyer who was on our board of directors. After showing the lawyer the letter, I told him I had done nothing wrong and I wasn't the least bit worried about it. "The truth will come out," I said. "I'm sure of that. I just don't know what to do. Nothing like this has ever happened to me."

He was an old mountain lawyer of about sixty-five. And if I thought he was going to pat my head and be sympathetic, I was wrong. Without warning, he slammed his hand on his desk and barked, "Sit down, sonny, and shut up!"

Stunned, I sat.

"Look," he rasped. "You are going to be facing a jury of twelve mountain men. And you are an outsider. Don't you forget it—*an outsider!* They'd just as soon hang you as look at you! If I were you, I'd give some serious thought to clearing out with my family. . . ."

I was shocked once again. This wasn't the counsel I expected. I told him I couldn't run away.

"Well then, let's just sit back and wait awhile and see what happens."

I left his office thinking, *Lord, if You want me in prison, then that's where I want to be. I've got two children now and I'd rather be with them and Carolyn. But I know You know what You're doing. I could be a missionary right there in jail. I just want to be in the center of Your will.*

I went to see Walter and told him what had happened. I felt it was time to have a meeting with the chairman of our board. Things had gone too far.

"Walter," I said, "we've never settled anything about those other allegations, either. Your father-in-law accused me and now these men are accusing me. I have a feeling there's a connection. . . ."

He looked at me for a minute, then his brow furrowed. "You know . . . come to think of it, my father-in-law gave T. J. and Horace some lumber and windows . . . about two weeks ago."

I recalled seeing lumber outside the cabin. "Why would he do a favor for a man who was just fired?" I asked.

Walter's eyes widened. It hit me at the same time: *Maybe the building materials were the payoff!*

Pop Claxton, evidently realizing I was doing too much digging and talking, may have put T. J. and Horace up to writing that letter, in hopes of scaring me enough to make me clear out.

Now it was Walter's turn to be stunned. "Ike," he said, "if this is true, it's going to ruin my family! But you're right . . . this thing has gotten out of hand. Sin cannot be swept under the rug." He looked away, then said, "This will just kill Margaret."

There was a maddening irony about the situation. Pop Claxton was, in many ways, a conscientious, caring man. He had worked hard to make the Mountain Haven Home what it was, and he and his wife were greatly respected in the community.

Yet this "good" man had an Achilles' heel, a weak spot that was his downfall: He was sexually attracted to young girls and acted out his sinful impulses instead of seeking spiritual counsel.

He was like many otherwise "good" people who are child molesters. They frequently have so many sterling qualities that you'd never dream there could be another side to them. And that's why they frequently get away with their crimes against children for as long as they do.

Because of Pop and Mom Claxton's accomplishments in the community—and the respect and prestige (and power) that went along with them—staff members were leary of challenging them in any way. This was the first time anyone had enough evidence against Pop.

Finally, Walter called the board chairman and filled him in. Then I called the chairman to tell him what I knew. There was to be a full-scale investigation of the allegations. A hearing was scheduled, with all board members to be in attendance.

In the meantime, news of T. J.'s allegations against me spread like wildfire through the countryside. At church, people came up to me and said, "Ike . . . we're behind you one hundred percent! We know you've done nothing wrong. And we're praying for you and your family."

The other staff and teachers rallied behind me, too. We held nightly prayer vigils that God would protect us, that the truth would come out, and that Pop Claxton would leave and the nightmare would be over.

What I did not know was that Pop had made his own accusations against me long before this time. He claimed I had been sexually abusing the children. And now he was in cahoots with the mountain men in a desperate bid to save himself.

The hearing was held at ten o'clock at night. All of the older girls were summoned to testify, one at a time, before the board. It was very secretive, and we were all praying fervently that the truth would prevail. Would the children speak the truth, or would their loyalty to Pop condemn me?

One by one, the girls began to testify to the board and answer questions. Finally it was Sarah's turn.

"Sarah Ann, did Mr. Keay ever . . . uh . . . touch you, or do anything not appropriate to you?"

"No, sir," she replied.

"Did he ever kiss or hug you?"

"Why, yes, sir . . . many times . . . but only in front of Mrs. Keay, or others. And in a nice way . . . real proper. He never touched me in the wrong way. And that's the truth."

"Well . . . did anybody else ever touch you . . . in a bad way? Now, this is very serious business and you must tell the truth. Don't be afraid."

"Well, sir . . . Pop Claxton . . . he fooled around with me. He used to take me into bed with him. And the other girls, too. Ask them. He's accusing Mr. Keay, but he's been doing it himself!"

The men looked at one another, shocked. More girls were brought in and questioned carefully. And one by one, they corroborated Sarah's testimony.

Thank God! After months of suspicion and accusations, the truth had finally come out.

It turned out that Pop had been molesting the girls at the home over a fifteen-year period. And, as that alumnus had confided, he allegedly abused some of the mothers of these girls!

But Pop Claxton was not an outsider. There would be no trial for him. Instead, he and his wife were ordered to pack up and clear out before daybreak. This was the way it was done in those days. Nobody wanted a court case; it would be bad publicity for the organization.

The board made another decision that night: Almost the entire staff would have to leave, partly to make a clean sweep and partly for reasons of safety. They were particularly concerned about my family.

"Ike," the chairman told me the next day, "you must take your family and leave Bitter Creek. We will not have your death on our hands . . . or the deaths of your family."

I was remembering what the lawyer had told me: *You are an outsider*.

I broke down and cried. Carolyn and I had come to nurture these kids, to care for them, to love them, in the Name of Christ. We had been so full of faith and hope then. And now, to be told we had to leave . . . it was too much.

You can imagine how the kids felt. They lost almost all the staff. Sin doesn't affect only the guilty; it affects everyone concerned.

Reluctantly, we packed our belongings in a U-Haul and headed back to St. Louis. George Stratton, who had also been let go, went with us.

As we bounced down that mountain road, I reminded myself that God had sent us there; now He would be calling us to a new work.

God had never let us down before; in my heart I was trusting Him for the future. It wasn't difficult because God was all we had. I recalled the words of Peter: "Lord, to whom shall we go? . . ." (John 6:68 KJV). To whom indeed?

We returned to St. Louis, hurting and confused. We were welcomed back by Jane and our church—and to the Evangelical Children's Home, as relief houseparents. Within a short time, George Stratton and Jane were married.

That summer I worked on renovating our church, Brentwood Bible. As I worked, pounding nails, cutting boards, laying shingles, suddenly the memory of that terrible night of the hearing would come back. I'd visualize those poor girls again, being questioned about shameful things. It made me angry and determined to do something about it—if not for those poor kids, then for other children.

But I felt if I were ever going to make a difference, I needed to have my own children's home. Only then could I implement my own ideas, introduce reforms, make sure kids were protected against child molesters. All that stood in the way was my lack of a degree. I had to get back to college . . . I had to finish my education.

In September 1963, I enrolled as a full-time student at Covenant College in St. Louis. I got a job doing maintenance work at the school in my spare time (in addition to being a relief houseparent at the Evangelical Children's Home). School was more difficult now, as I became a father once again. This time it was a boy—a direct answer to prayer. We gave him the good

Scottish name of Brian, which in Gaelic means "strong." We wanted him to be strong for the Lord.

There were now five of us to feed and, as a full-time student, I couldn't work enough hours to make ends meet.

One day, we ran out of food; the cupboards literally were bare. I reminded the Lord that it was His responsibility to meet our needs.

I went to a wedding reception that evening, and one of the school's bookkeepers asked me, "Ike, have you seen the check that came in for you today?"

Praise God—a check for four hundred dollars! It was a direct confirmation of Philippians 4:19: "My God shall supply all your need . . ." (KJV).

God was mysteriously at work again. In January 1964, I heard that Covenant was considering separating the college from the seminary. The seminary would stay in St. Louis, but there was talk about purchasing a large hotel in Chattanooga, Tennessee, as a new site for the college.

I talked with my good friend Ed Steele, the school's business manager, and asked him if he would check and see if there were any children's homes in the Chattanooga area where I could work while finishing my education.

That was when we heard about Bethel Bible School.

15. Full Circle

You intended to harm me, but God intended it for good to accomplish what is now being done, the saving of many lives.

Genesis 50:20 NIV

And so we came to Bethel.

At long last, my dream had come true: I was the director (acting) of a children's home! Finally, a place where I could put into practice the things I had learned growing up in a home and from working in child care; not only the pitfalls but the positive things as well. Best of all, it would give me a really free hand in presenting Jesus Christ to these hurting kids, and I would not have to explain or apologize for that to anyone. (This, in fact, was the purpose of Bethel Bible School.)

For years I had been convinced that in the final analysis (after the psychologists and teachers and child experts have had their input), ultimately Jesus is the only One who can make these young, broken lives whole again. And I was just as convinced that without Jesus, no matter what else is done for them, these needy children will never be whole persons.

If this was true at Bonnie Brae Farm and the Mountain Haven Home, it was even more true for Bethel Bible School, because *all of the children at Bethel were the children of prisoners.* That meant that either the mother or the father (or both) had committed a crime and was serving time. Not only had these children been forcibly separated from their parents but also, in most cases, they had seen family violence (even the murder of one parent by the other), or were themselves victims of sexual or physical abuse.

Sexual abuse, drunkenness, drug addiction, neglect, hunger, brutality, murder—these kids had seen or been the victims of cruelty and depravity. If any children ever needed Jesus Christ, these children did.

What a privilege and a challenge that God had led me to Bethel. In ministering to these hurting kids, *I would be ministering to the child I had been*. I felt as if I had indeed come full circle. I had come home.

Carolyn seemed content: After all, we were finally ensconced in the director's home—the most spacious and substantial house we had ever lived in, with four small bedrooms and two baths. It seemed like a palace to us.

But if my dear wife thought she was going to be the mistress of the manse and a full-time mother to our three active youngsters (and pregnant with our fourth), she was mistaken. There was no secretary at Bethel, and Carolyn was told she was "it." That wasn't all: She was also expected to take charge of the clothing room, the toy room, and the doling out of the children's allowances. Besides those jobs, the telephone for the whole complex was routed through our house, so Carolyn was taking all the incoming calls.

At first I had my office in the house, so Carolyn did my typing and a bit of bookkeeping, until I was able to hire a secretary. She also agreed to handle the home's birthday parties, but rather than have one big party each month, we decided on individual parties for each child.

The only meal Carolyn was required to make was breakfast, since lunch and dinner were served at the main dining hall. Once Kim, Debbie, and Brian got there, however, they weren't interested in eating. All they wanted to do was look at the other children. Like the other staff, we had some of the Bethel children at our table, so Carolyn was not only responsible for feeding her own brood but also the others.

On May 17, 1965, our answer to prayer was born—a second son, to whom we gave another good Scottish name—Alan, meaning "laughter." We wanted him to bring joy to people. Now our family was complete.

* * *

When we first came to Bethel, meals were served cafeteria style, which is about as far from a family setting as one can get. I quickly changed it to family-style service.

There were some complaints that there were now a lot more dishes to wash, since each table had to have serving bowls. But I pointed out that it was a small price to pay for a warmer, family feeling, with the staff and children gathering for real, sit-down meals.

It was not my intention to make changes simply for the sake of change, or to let everyone know I was the boss. Every change was made after much soul-searching and prayer, with the idea of increasing a family feeling at Bethel, or to benefit the children in some way. And before each change I gave the staff ample notice, to allow for input and discussion.

For instance, right after we arrived, we found that at our Sunday-morning services (we had our own church on campus), a dear lady would stand up and ask each person, "How many times did you read your Bible this week?"

"Seven times" . . . "seven times" . . . "seven times" . . . etc., etc., everyone would say, as she went around the congregation. And this wonderful Christian lady actually accepted what she was hearing. Everyone was *so* devout!

Not only did it take forever to go around the group but we knew some of those children (and maybe the staff members) were telling, shall I say, "untruths" about the frequency of their Bible readings.

Since we Keays were still getting settled in, we weren't having our daily devotions as frequently as we would have under normal circumstances. So when it came to the director's family, either Carolyn or I would say, "Three times," or five times, or whatever. We thought it was more important to be honest than consistent. But this disclosure would be met by a holy hush, or more accurately, a stony silence.

Finally I said, "Now look, gang, it's real important that we read God's Word every day, but it's also important that we be truthful. If you've read your Bibles only once a week, or even not at all, be honest and say what you really did . . . or didn't do. It's more important to tell the truth than to try to look good."

Immediately after I gave this pep talk, we went around the room again and the replies were startlingly different: "One time" . . . "four times" . . . "zero times" . . . but oh, how refreshingly honest!

Very soon, we eliminated this questionable exercise entirely.

Another problem was that every other Sunday there were three services: morning, noon, and evening. As if that weren't enough, on Sunday evenings, there was a full hour of Bible reading, without an iota of comment or interpretation! In the summer there were additional services during the week.

I felt that all of these services were just too much, particularly for children. I can't think of a quicker way to turn kids off to Jesus and the things of God than to constantly force-feed them great chunks of Scripture with no commentary.

In addition to worship services and Bible reading, the Bethel children were memorizing anywhere from five to fifteen Bible verses a week. They had competitions among themselves and at Bible Memorization Association Camp, where they would be given awards for their memory work.

When I began teaching the high school Sunday-school class, I found the kids knew more Scripture than most pastors—chapter upon chapter, verbatim!

But there was something about all this biblical knowledge that bothered me. So I tried an experiment. . . .

One day in Sunday school I asked a sixteen-year-old boy to quote Galatians 2:20. He did it—flawlessly: "I am crucified with Christ: nevertheless I live; yet not I, but Christ liveth in me: and the life which I now live . . ." (KJV).

"Now Johnny," I said, "what do you think that means?"

"Uh . . . ah . . . ummmm . . . I'm not sure, Mr. Keay. I, er . . . I really don't know."

And none of the other kids were sure what it meant, either.

I could accept the well-meant rationale behind all the memory work: Even though the children might not fully understand the verses now, they would later in life. It was important to instill Scripture in them while they were young, before they left Bethel and went out into the world—so the argument went. But I would rather have a child memorize one verse a week and be able to apply it in his or her life than have him remember reams of verses that mean nothing.

I felt changes were in order. First, we eliminated a few of the church services, reducing the Sunday schedule to just two. Next, we stopped the long, uninterrupted Bible reading entirely. We kept the memorization program because we believed in it, but we cut back, giving the children fewer verses to digest weekly.

Surprisingly, I didn't get too much flak about these changes, but there was one area with which I did have trouble. It was in regard to the dress code. As at Mountain Haven Home, the girls at Bethel were required to wear dresses at all times—even when they were working in the garden or climbing on the monkey bars. When I announced an impending change in the dress code, allowing shorts and slacks for the girls (as long as they weren't too tight, short, or otherwise immodest), there was resistance.

It was understandable. Bethel was and is a conservative Christian home, and the dress code stressed modesty. However, I argued, there is nothing modest about a girl leaning over picking vegetables or swinging upside down from the jungle gym, showing her underwear.

Liberalizing the dress code was nothing compared to what I felt had to be done next.

Bethel, as I've indicated, had a school right on campus, with grades one through eight. Brother Hipp's strong desire was to give the children a good Christian education. Although our teachers were excellent, the school's physical plant left a great deal to be desired. School was held in the basement of the chapel: four little rooms, each housing two grades. There were children with IQs of 50 to 100 in the same classroom.

The kids would be pulled out of class to help unload hay, wash dishes, peel potatoes, or other "emergencies." (There simply weren't enough adult staff members to handle all the chores.) Consequently, there was little motivation. The message being delivered to the children was, "Learning is okay, as long as there's nothing really important to be done." So, the kids didn't care.

"But these are damaged children, Ike," staffers protested when I broached the subject of closing the school. "They need special handling, which they will not get in outside schools."

"They also need to be prepared to face the outside world," I countered. "These kids need to interact with all kinds of people and situations. They're too isolated here. They cannot be little hothouse plants."

I felt that on a number of counts, we simply weren't meeting the educational needs of children who had two strikes against them already.

Our biggest problem was the fact that our school failed the state inspection each year, though we were given a temporary license to continue—provided we could begin solving the problem of the physical plant. The truth was that we really couldn't afford to have our own school. We didn't have adequate funding to run both a school and a home, and the home was more important.

The possibility of closing the school caused hurt feelings among the teaching staff, but I had to think of the children's best interests. In 1965 the board, with mixed emotions, agreed with me to close the school, and we began sending our children to Tennessee Temple Christian Schools in Chattanooga.

Bethel had almost no recreation program. Swings, a jungle gym, and a few horses were about it. So we brought in a full recreational program with all types of contests, such as horseshoes, volleyball, etc. We also had major sports: baseball, basketball, track, football. We even had a trampoline.

We set up the kids in teams: the Blues and the Whites (Bethel's colors). Not only did we get the kids competing among themselves but we also set up basketball and baseball games with other schools and homes. This new athletic program was healthy for the children, and it increased their feeling of togetherness and pride in Bethel.

As you might imagine, most of our changes caused the children to breathe a sigh of relief. They were delighted, and who could blame them? They had less memory work, a reasonable amount of church and Sunday school, a sports program, and eventually were able to go to school in town.

One other change I made after the first year was to close our church on campus and encourage the staff and children to go to local churches. I wanted them to be part of local congregations like normal families.

I don't mean to give the impression that Bethel was a bad place when I arrived and that I single-handedly turned everything around. That is not at all true. Bethel Bible School was a home that had been struggling for years to provide prisoners' children with adequate care—shelter, clothing, school, and three square meals a day.

True, the changes I was introducing were many and far reaching, but I could heartily agree with that great missionary statesman William Carey, who said, "Expect great things from God and attempt great things for God." That was how I interpreted my role at Bethel. Indeed, I had a strong conviction that all of the changes were what God intended for Bethel, and I would have been remiss had I done any less.

Still, what I didn't realize when I first came was that even though the board had agreed to let me be acting director, they were still hoping to find that man with the master's degree. If and when they found him, they planned to keep me on as assistant director.

At the end of six months, much to my pleasure, the board made me the full-fledged director.

My dream was finally realized.

16. Scotty and Me

A friend loves at all times,
and a brother is born for adversity.

Proverbs 17:17 NIV

Thank God for Scott Probosco. I'm convinced that the Lord, knowing things at Bethel Bible Village (as it is now known) would not be easy, prepared the way before me by putting Scotty in a position of power and authority as chairman of the board of directors. Without Scotty's strong and outspoken support and his friendship, I doubt I would have lasted a year at Bethel.

All the men on Bethel's board were good, God-fearing, solid Christians who were committed to helping the children. Yet not all of them had my particular vision for the future of Bethel, and many of them disagreed with my methods. Then there was Scotty. . . .

Scotty and I were "in sync." He trusted me and believed in what I was trying to accomplish for Bethel, even those times when I came off to those godly but tough-minded board members as a starry-eyed dreamer who was shooting himself (and Bethel, in the process) in the foot. It almost seemed that Scotty was waiting for someone like me to come along, to help focus and ignite his own goals for Bethel. Indeed, the vision that God had given me for Bethel turned out to be Scotty's, as well.

Scott Probosco, a tall, athletic-looking man with brown hair and a handsome face, is a respected and beloved citizen of Chattanooga. Although today he is enjoying a well-earned retirement, when I came to Bethel in 1964, he was the vice-chairman of Chattanooga's American National Bank, which had been founded by his grandfather and father. And though he is the picture of dignity with his conservative suits and trademark bow ties, everyone in town calls him "Scotty."

In spite of his wealth and position, Scotty makes *everybody* feel like *somebody.* One of the first times I visited him, he was showing me around the bank and introduced me to one of the guards. He treated the man as if he were head of security at the White House.

But Scotty Probosco is not a mere flatterer; when he says something nice about you, you know he means it. A Christian gentleman who lives his faith, Scotty has a way of making the humblest person feel valued, because he really loves people. And that's the secret of his popularity.

From the start, Scotty backed me.

At first I wasn't on a budget because the board was in the process of drawing up a new one. But budget or no budget, the home was always on the brink of financial disaster. Bethel was and is dependent mainly on private contributions from concerned individuals. Back in 1964 we needed miracles, and I expected them. In the meantime, I was always trying to figure out ways to increase our income, to feed and clothe the children, and improve their quality of life.

A few board members reasoned that since almost anything was better than what these poor kids had before coming to Bethel, why extend ourselves to do even more? I disagreed. I had been a deprived child myself, and I was determined to do more.

First, I had gas pumps installed for our vehicles, to cut costs. There weren't too many rumblings about that because the installation was free (we paid only for the fuel). The savings were immediately evident.

But that was only the start. Those kids' beds. . . . From the first time Brother Hipp showed us through the boys' dorm, the sight of those little army cots with their gray blankets made me wince. I was remembering our beds at Bonnie Brae, with their sagging springs. So I bought fifty army hospital beds, very substantial, with good springs. A manufacturer donated the mattresses.

When we closed the school, we converted the former teachers' residence into a cottage for eight boys—a preview of things to come. Not only did we buy furniture but we also remodeled the place. We tore out walls, improved the wiring, and expanded the bathroom facilities. And of course we had to hire additional staff.

I ordered a new van . . . there was so much that needed to be done with that old campus.

Yet, for most of these changes and improvements, I seldom went to the board and asked for money. I just went out and bought things. I was trusting the Lord to supply all our needs at Bethel. When I saw that something needed to be fixed or purchased, I usually consulted only Him.

Unknown to me, some board members were hitting Scotty with criticism about my expenditures, because it was he who had told me to "run with the ball" . . . and I was running. I was getting a reputation of being a big spender.

Then came the matter of the printing press. . . .

After six months at the home, I saw that Bethel was spending an awful lot of money having letters, brochures, and fliers printed. I got a very good deal on a printing press for four thousand dollars.

At our next board meeting, the members were looking over the treasurer's report.

"What in Sam Hill is this item here . . . four thousand dollars for a printing press? *Who* ordered a printing press?" The speaker was Percy Dedweiler, a tough-minded attorney who, like many self-made men, had a tight fist with a dollar. And he knew all too well who had ordered the printing press.

"I did, Percy," I replied. "We're spending hundreds of dollars on outside printing. With this printing press, we'll actually be saving money. And besides, we can train some of the kids in printing. It's a very useful trade."

"Why don't you come to us when you need something—and

ask?" he inquired. "We have something to say about this kind of thing, you know."

"Perhaps I should have," I replied. "I did . . . uh . . . pray about it."

Dedweiler shifted in his seat. "That's all well and good, Ike," he replied, "but this is our business, too. This board's function is to approve expenditures. Now before you spend this kind of money, we want you to get approval from the executive committee."

He looked around. Other board members were nodding in agreement.

Then Scotty spoke. "I think we all appreciate the fact that Ike is working hard, trying to find ways to cut costs," he said in a calm voice. "And I'd like to suggest that he still be able to spend for routine, day-to-day items without bothering us. We don't want to hamstring him . . . I suggest a $500 limit. For anything over that, he'll ask the executive committee. Is that okay with you gentlemen . . . Ike?"

The board and I agreed. Thanks to Scotty, I still had some financial autonomy.

Gradually, God showed me that what worked financially in my personal life didn't necessarily work in corporate life. He showed me that it was the board's legitimate function to decide financial matters, and we had to work together. I was learning. . . .

Remodeling and buying equipment to save a few dollars was like putting Band-Aids on gunshot wounds. Very quickly I perceived that something more drastic was needed to pull Bethel out of the malaise from which it suffered. The real problem with Bethel was its physical plant and location.

To see the houseparents struggling with too many children in our big dormitories was disheartening and demoralizing—and pretty near impossible for them. But soon after I arrived, Brother Hipp and the board started laying plans to build another dormitory, which would house sixty children!

Three months after I arrived at Bethel, I visited Scotty at the bank. He greeted me warmly in his handsomely furnished office and asked me to sit down.

After a few amenities, I came right to the point: "Scotty, we need to move our campus off the mountain and build a new campus closer to town."

I thought he was going to choke. "Move the campus!" he sputtered, almost leaping out of his chair. Then looking to make sure no one had heard, he whispered, "Close the door! This is heresy!"

I quickly got up, closed the door, and returned to my seat.

"Ike . . . why do you want to do that?" he said, leaning forward. "Brother Hipp has worked so hard on this place! Why, he built some of those buildings with his own hands! And our contributors have given thousands of dollars to maintain it. We can't just . . . move!"

"I know all that . . . and yes, we can," I replied. "God was with Brother Hipp in a mighty way when he built Bethel. And I can imagine what it cost him in blood, sweat, and tears. But now something better is needed, Scotty. Up north, they stopped building these big dorms twenty-five years ago. The thing now is family-style cottages, with no more than eight or ten kids to a house."

He had stopped fidgeting and was listening.

"Scotty . . . we have to stress quality, not quantity. You've got four kids, right? How would you like to try to take care of twenty-five kids . . . get them up in the morning, make sure they wash, comb their hair, shine their shoes. Well, that's what our houseparents have to do. And there's no way one couple can care properly for that many kids. All kids need individual attention. We're herding them like—like cattle! And now our board's talking about an even larger dorm? When Brother Hipp first showed me those plans I told him I just couldn't go along with that."

"You told him that? Ike . . . Brother Hipp has his heart set on this big dorm. He *wants* to take in even more kids. So maybe we have to sacrifice quality a little. . . ."

"I know he loves the children," I replied. "He'd take every

stray child off the street if he could. But Scotty, these kids need to be in smaller cottages that are similar to real homes. They've got to have more individual attention—plus the fact that Bethel's too . . . isolated. Our kids . . . we're keeping them hidden up there. They need to be part of a community to which they'll eventually be returning.

"And you know yourself that every year Bethel's been failing the Welfare Department's standards. They've just been patient with us year after year. . . ."

Scotty looked at me, analyzing every word I was saying.

"We have septic tank problems, wiring problems, problems of overcrowding," I continued. "We've got to correct all those problems anyway, Scotty. In my opinion this would be a good time to move our campus and build it the way it ought to be."

In the end, Scotty had to agree with me. He suggested we check out some other properties closer to town. "How many acres do you figure we'll need?"

"A hundred, at least,"

He sucked in his breath. "Ike, it's going to cost a lot of money. And we'll have to sell our current property. . . ." He paused a moment, then said, "Look, we'll work on the board together, but let's take it easy. Don't say anything until the two of us have checked this out a bit. We don't want to go to the board without some facts and figures."

Scotty and I quietly began looking around on weekends. I prayed a lot, too.

Then came the meeting at which the board was going to decide about the big new dormitory. We couldn't wait any longer. I was so grateful the Lord had given me a friend and supporter like Scotty.

There was a bit of discussion and then Scotty took the floor. "Gentlemen," he began, "Ike and I have been talking. He's the professional in child care, and he feels very strongly that we've got to have fewer kids, not more, per building. I agree with him. I have my hands full with four. I don't know how our houseparents can do a proper job with twenty-five or thirty. It's humanly impossible. I agree with Ike that what we need are smaller, family-style cottages, with about eight or ten children in each."

"Do you know what that'll cost?" Percy Dedweiler snapped.

"A lot of money, Percy, a lot of money," Scotty replied. Dead silence.

"Furthermore," Scotty continued, dropping his bombshell, "our campus is too isolated. I know we have a lot invested in it and it has served its purpose well, until now. But for the sake of our Bethel children, who must one day return to society, we have to move closer to town. We've got to be near community resources—schools, churches, shopping centers."

This announcement was met with expressions of shock and bewilderment. Scotty called for order and rehearsed all our arguments for moving the campus.

When he finished, one of the men cleared his throat and said, "Look, Scotty, what you're talking about will cost thousands of dollars, which we don't have. And let me remind you, these are prisoners' kids. They don't need much . . . shirts on their backs, food in their stomachs, and a place to sleep. They don't need nice things. They don't need that kind of attention. All they need is the basics. It's better than living out in some little shack."

I was shocked. "Steve," I said, "how would you like that for your own children?"

"Ike," he said, eyes flashing, "these are not my kids! They are *prisoners'* kids!"

"Well," I insisted, "they *could* be your kids."

You could have cut the tension with a knife. Then someone cleared his throat and said, "All that aside . . . we simply don't have the money to buy a new property."

"Gentlemen," I said, "if this is God's will—that we move our campus—then He will supply the money we need. And if we don't have the faith, and if we can't provide properly for these kids, why then . . . *we ought to get out of the child-care business!*"

After another moment of strained silence, Percy Dedweiler said, "Let's hear what Brother Hipp has to say." He knew the founder's opinion would end all discussion of this foolishness.

The room was dead quiet. I had been wondering (fearfully, I might add) what Brother Hipp's reaction would be. Would he think it was heresy? That we were traitors? He had sat quietly through the whole discussion, head slightly bowed, listening. I sent up a quick prayer.

"You know," he began, in his thoughtful way, "I have been going to prisons for many years. Some states are building beautiful, brand-new prisons . . . for criminals. Here we have these innocent children, and if they're building big, beautiful buildings for prisoners, why can't we have beautiful buildings for our children? This is God's work. 'With man this is impossible, but with God all things are possible' [Matthew 19:26 NIV].

"Scotty . . . Ike," he said, looking at us, "that sounds good to me. I want the best for these children. They deserve it. As for moving the campus . . . well, I'd miss this old place, but I'm open to the Lord's leading on that, too."

Had I been sitting next to Brother Hipp, I would have hugged him! Praise God for this courageous, selfless servant of the Lord. Tears were in my eyes. . . .

The upshot was that the board gave me permission to check out other homes in various parts of the country, to determine the best design for a cottage to house eight children. I was even given a special airline ticket that enabled me to fly all over during the summer of 1965. I flew out to Boys Town in Nebraska and up to the Milton Hershey Home in Hershey, Pennsylvania, among others. Not only did I talk to the directors, but I also talked to houseparents and maintenance men. I asked them what things worked in cottage design and what didn't—what kind of heating, lighting, how many closets, and so on.

When I finally returned to Bethel, I got together with Scotty and an architect and we drew up plans for a prototype cottage. It wasn't easy. If it were all on one floor, the place would be too spread out for the houseparents to keep track of the kids. But if it were on two floors, they wouldn't have good control either. The solution was a split-level design.

There would be four bedrooms for the children (two kids to a room) and two bathrooms; an apartment for the houseparents (a home within a home—two bedrooms, a living room, a hideaway kitchen, and a bathroom); a large kitchen; a spacious living room; and downstairs, a recreation room with Ping-Pong tables and other equipment, plus a room and a bath for relief houseparents. There would be a total of fourteen rooms, covering fifty-four hundred square feet. The projected cost was about fifty thousand dollars for each cottage.

Of course, we had not a penny to build the first cottage—and I envisioned at least twelve. Before we could do anything, we had to move. Scotty and I continued to scour the countryside within a forty-mile radius of Chattanooga, looking at farms with large tracts of land of one hundred acres or more that were up for sale. We looked for almost four years without success.

In the meantime, our old property was up for sale, but no one seemed interested. Everyone was saying we had a white elephant up there on the mountain. Not only was it too isolated but our buildings weren't so great and there was no nearby river or lake for recreation to make it attractive as a camp or school. The board had steadfastly refused to purchase a new campus until we sold our old campus.

On a cold day in February 1968, I requested an early-morning meeting of the board and told them, "Gentlemen, we have to make our move."

"Ike, we agree," Percy Dedweiler said. "So whenever the Lord helps us sell this place, we'll have the money to move, and not before."

"I must say what's heavy on my heart," I replied. "I see a lack of faith here. We must act first . . . step out, demonstrate our faith. Then the Lord will get us a buyer."

"Totally impractical!" someone snapped.

"It's biblical," I countered. Then I gave them the argument that had convinced Scotty Probosco: "Do you remember when the children of Israel were about to cross over the Jordan into the Promised Land? Well, the waters of the Jordan didn't part while they waited on the bank. It wasn't until the priests stepped out in faith, gentlemen, *and the soles of their sandals touched the top of the water, that it parted!*"

I had them turn to the passage in Joshua 3, and we read it. "Gentlemen," I said, holding up my Bible, "I'm here to tell you that we need that same kind of bold faith!"

There was coughing and shuffling of papers. Scotty's eyes were shining.

"I have here a list of Bible verses about faith and trust." I passed out mimeographed pages on which I had eight or ten verses. Then I went over those verses with them, one by one.

Scripture is so powerful to convince. Most of those tough-minded, pragmatic businessmen were won over by those verses. But the holdouts warned that if we bought a new property and were unable to sell the old one, and it went to wrack and ruin, it would be a poor example of stewardship.

"God will not allow that to happen," I said. "God is going to sell that place for us before we ever move into a new place."

"Gentlemen," Scotty said, "we've been waiting four years and it hasn't worked. It's about time we stepped out in faith. If we do, God is going to part the waters, just as we read here this morning. I suggest we go ahead and do it."

The upshot was that the board finally voted to buy a property (if and when we found one!) even before we sold our campus and had the money. We began our hunt again in earnest.

Meanwhile, how to sell that property? "Lord . . . I've stuck my neck out," I prayed. There had to be a way. I thought the best prospect would be a church looking for a summer camp. But who would be interested if there was no lake or river?

God doesn't always speak directly; He also gives us creative ideas. Within two weeks, an idea came to me: *We've got this section over here . . . a deep hollow in the land. And we've got plenty of springs. My buddy Dan has a bulldozer . . . how much would it cost to put a lake in there?*

Dan did it for a super price; he bulldozed a twenty-five-foot deep, three-acre lake for forty-five hundred dollars.

While the lake was filling, we continued to hunt for a property. Someone said, "Listen . . . there's a doctor who has a farm in Hixson. His children are getting older and will soon be leaving home. He and his wife can't possibly take care of all those cows by themselves. Maybe he'd be interested in selling."

It was only sixty-seven acres, but it was right on a creek and close to town. So, we approached the doctor. To my surprise, he said he was interested. The only problem was his asking price: He would sell the land, his house and barns, and his cattle to us for $155,000, which was a very reasonable price. When I told him I'd have to take it to my board, he warned me that was his best price. He wouldn't come down another penny.

The board said, "Go back to him and tell him we'll give him one hundred and twenty-five thousand dollars."

"Gentlemen, he won't come down any more. You're wasting my time and his."

"Well, you go back. That's all we'll offer."

Reluctantly, I went back to the doctor.

"Look, Ike," he said with some exasperation, "I told you one hundred and fifty-five thousand dollars and not a penny less. I'm going to give you one week to decide, or it's no deal!"

I left that meeting discouraged, praying, "God, after four years of searching, I know this is the place You've chosen for Bethel. . . ."

It was Good Friday. Where was I going to get an additional thirty thousand dollars in one week? I stayed up all night, praying and seeking God's will. Toward morning He put an idea in my mind: *Write an article to the people of Chattanooga about your need and take it to the newspapers.*

Of course! But I'd have to get the article to the paper that morning if it were going to make the Sunday edition. There was no time to consult the board.

"Lord . . . I've just got to be sure this is what You want. If this article appears and the board members see in the newspapers that Bethel needs thirty thousand dollars, they'll say, 'What's this guy doing?' "

I opened my Bible and began my normal reading for the day. The passage happened to be the one in which Jesus said to Peter, "I have prayed for thee, that thy faith fail not . . ." (Luke

22:32 KJV). And I knew the message was for me. Jesus was praying for me, too, *that my faith would not fail.*

I got a pen and paper and spent the rest of the night writing an article. In the morning I took it to both newspapers in town.

That Easter Sunday, Chattanoogans saw the following front-page headline in the *Chattanooga News–Free Press:*

BETHEL BIBLE SCHOOL
NEEDS MONEY FAST
Director Confident
Funds Will Appear

The article read in part:

> The Bethel Bible School on Signal Mountain has one week in which to raise an additional $30,000, which will enable the school to buy some 70 acres near Chickamauga Lake to build enlarged and improved facilities, Ike Keay, the school director, said today.
>
> Mr. Keay has no idea where the money is coming from, but he is confident it will be provided. What makes him so sure? "The same thing that has kept the school going for some 14 years," he said with a smile, "and that's faith. . . .
>
> "I personally believe that God, through the people of Chattanooga, will supply our need," Mr. Keay stated. He urged everyone to mention this need to their Sunday school classes, church, business and civic groups this week. . . .
>
> As an example of faith, Mr. Keay said that the operating funds of the school had been depleted recently until there was only $27 in the bank. "We weren't worried," he said, "because we had faith the Lord would provide just as He promised. He always comes through to supply our needs, and I'm just as certain He'll supply the money this week needed to buy the property."

On Monday morning I received a call from the doctor. "Ike, I see now that you really mean business. Don't worry about the Friday deadline. You take all the time you need."

The Lord was working mightily. Contributions began to pour in. By Friday, the day of the original deadline, the dear people of Chattanooga had sent us thousands of dollars . . . I wasn't sure how much because it was still coming in, but it wasn't the thirty-thousand dollars I had asked for. I was a bit disappointed.

Although the doctor had given me an extension, the Lord laid it on my heart to go see him. We talked a bit, and then he said, "I'll tell you what . . . I'll sell the cattle myself, separately. You can have the property for one hundred and forty-five thousand dollars. Do you think you can swing that?"

I thanked him and went home . . . praying. The board was prepared to offer $125,000 . . . the doctor had come down $10,000 . . . which meant we needed an additional $20,000. We didn't have that much in contributions.

Back at my office, I counted the money again. A few additional contributions had come in while I was out. As I began opening the letters, I saw there might be more than I had expected. There were three checks for $100 each. That gave us a total of $18,000. There was a money order for almost $500. That gave us $18,500. I began to sweat. Another envelope revealed a check for $1,000. That gave us $19,500! There were a couple of checks for $50 . . . then five letters with $25 each, making $19,725 . . . and contributions of $5 and $10. . . .

I sat there with the checks spread before me; tears were in my eyes. The total had come to just a little over twenty thousand dollars . . . *the exact amount we needed!* I was utterly overwhelmed by the Lord's goodness. The thirty thousand dollars hadn't come in as I had expected, so once again the Lord showed me He is in control of things.

But the miracle didn't stop there.

Scotty said, "I have an aunt who would probably give us some money to build a cottage. Let's name the doctor's house after my aunt, Margaret Morrison. We'll call it Morrison Cottage, and we can use the fifty thousand dollars for our down payment on the property."

Eight months after buying the property, in April 1969, we began building our five new cottages, plus the director's home. (Of course, when we began building, we still hadn't sold our old campus, so we were trusting the Lord.)

The five cottages were going to cost $250,000, and we had no money. Again, as we stepped out in faith and began to build, the Lord began to act. Not only did Margaret Morrison give us a cottage but the Exchange Club also gave us one. A foundation gave us money for two other cottages and roads . . . someone put on a roof free . . . then a local firm put on another roof . . . a board member gave us carpeting for two cottages . . . Modern Maid gave us all our kitchens. People were just super.

But midway in the construction, we ran out of cash again. In fact, we were seventy thousand dollars in the hole. And even though the board had given me the go-ahead to build those cottages, Percy Dedweiler climbed all over me at the next meeting.

"We told you not to spend money you didn't have! You were to come to us first!"

"Percy," I replied, "you told me a year ago *you* were going to give me a cottage!"

He shifted in his seat. "I am not giving you that money until the stock market goes up!"

"But Percy . . . you promised me you would give me fifty-thousand dollars last year."

"You heard me . . . I'm not giving you that money until the market goes up. And that's final!"

"Okay . . . you've been waiting a year for the market to go up on that stock and it hasn't budged? Now we're going to *pray* for that stock market to go *up*."

Every day a number of us prayed about it. The market began to go up . . . and up . . . and up. In two weeks Percy sold his stock for what he wanted and gave us the promised money.

(Praise God for Percy! Through him, the Lord taught me you can be on opposite sides of the fence and yet love one another.)

What do you suppose happened next? After Percy gave us our money, the stock went right down to the cellar again!

On November 7, 1969, we moved.

What a mammoth job that was—moving more than one hundred people with all their clothes and household goods! Everybody pitched in, even our littlest kids. In fact, moving Bethel became a community project. Hundreds of people joined us for the big move, loading up trucks and cars and hauling us down the mountain. It was exhausting but exhilarating.

It was bittersweet, too: Old Bethel, our Mountain Miracle for fifteen years, had been born of Brother Hipp's faith, love, and toil and had served its purpose well. As we drove down the mountain for the last time, I'm sure there were some tears shed.

To add to our joy, just three days before the move we finally sold our Signal Mountain campus. (We got $150,000 for the old place and had paid $145,000 for the new place. So we had a $5,000 profit, which more than paid for the man-made lake!) Now we could complete the first stage of our new building program.

After years of being good but cautious men, our Bethel board had stepped out in faith. And when they did, God came through for us in a wonderful way!

"This is the Lord's doing; it is marvellous in our eyes" (Psalms 118:23 KJV).

17. The Children of Bethel

And they brought young children to him, that he should touch them: and his disciples rebuked those that brought them. But when Jesus saw it, he was much displeased, and said unto them, Suffer the little children to come unto me, and forbid them not: for of such is the kingdom of God. . . . And he took them up in his arms, put his hands upon them, and blessed them.

Mark: 10:13–16 KJV

Until 1954, when Brother Hipp found that family of six hungry, neglected kids living under a tree and started Bethel, there had not been one home in the entire United States exclusively for prisoners' children—a place where they could be taken in and cared for when violence tore their families apart.

Back in the 1940s, long before he founded Bethel, Brother Hipp saw three little innocent children in a filthy jail cell with their mother. The children were with her in that terrible place because no one cared enough to provide a decent home for them.

The Lord used that heartrending image to plant a seed in Brother Hipp's heart that was to come to fruition ten years later, when he founded Bethel for the forgotten children of crime.

Every child needs to be able to look up to his or her mother and father, to think they are "the greatest." Children need sound parental role models on which to pattern themselves. When these models are warped or lacking, children are damaged mentally, emotionally, and spiritually.

Invariably, visitors to Bethel remark about our younger children and how really beautiful they are. To see these little ones, so healthy looking, rosy cheeks and shiny hair, laughing and playing like any other children, getting ready for school, doing homework, or listening to a Bible story, you would never dream of the horrors they have witnessed. Some of these little ones have seen one of their parents murder the other.

After the crime, these children see their homes invaded by police and their surviving parent handcuffed and taken away to prison.

And before that crime is ever committed, many of our children have been neglected and/or abused by parents who in many instances were themselves abused as children and who may be addicted to alcohol or drugs, or might be career criminals. I remember three towheaded little boys, ages five to eight, who had been so deprived and so neglected that they had never learned to speak. Another family of children lived in a chicken coop, sleeping on the floor—a hard, foul bed of encrusted chicken droppings. We had a five-year-old girl who ate from dumpsters. We also had a set of twins who saw their father kill their mother with an ax.

Nearly all of our girls, and some of our boys, have been sexually abused by their own fathers, stepfathers, or other male relatives or neighbors. Frequently, the sexual abuse of a Bethel child is the crime for which the parent has been imprisoned. In some instances women, upon learning their husbands have sexually abused their daughters, take the law into their own hands and kill their spouses. And when they are sent to prison, Bethel makes a home for their children.

The child, needing to look up to the parent, often cannot deal with the terrible reality of what that parent has done to her or him. A child unconsciously exalts his mother as an ideal woman. So he subconsciously reasons, "When Mommy gets drunk and screams and hits me, *she* can't be bad. *I* must be bad." And the child's psyche is damaged, sometimes beyond human healing.

The same reaction holds true with regard to an abusive father, whom the child needs to see as the provider and strong protector. When that protector betrays the child's trust. . . .

Children's homes are filled with the living, devastating results of parental abuse, and experts say that child abuse is on the rise in America. At Bethel Bible Village, we are trying, by the grace of God, to salvage the broken lives of these victims of crime before they in turn become crime or suicide statistics.

Typically, children are remanded to us by the courts, by

human services agencies, or by relatives when the parents are jailed. Sometimes the parent still at home is emotionally unable to cope with the trauma of the spouse's crime or has no means of support, so we have to take the children.

I was at Bonnie Brae for nine years. Today, under new state guidelines, children are not to be institutionalized for more than eighteen months. Because their parents are serving sentences, the average stay of a Bethel child is two to three years.

That is why in the time we have them, we do our utmost to help these children heal, to provide an education, to give them skills and discipline and self-respect. We try to show them by word and example that no matter how terrible their home lives might have been, a loving God is with them every step of the way; they are valued and can make something of their lives. Even when they leave, if they have problems "making it," we'll take them back to offer them a shoulder to lean (or cry) on, and food and shelter—a chance to regroup before trying again.

We wouldn't hope to attempt this herculean task in our own knowledge and strength, for we would surely fail. But through patient kindness and nurture, we try to demonstrate for these hurting children the love of Christ, and hopefully, introduce them to Him. Most of the time we succeed, but not always. We keep trying, because He will go with them when they leave this haven.

Indeed, the motto of Bethel Bible Village is: *Preventing crime by presenting Christ.*

The following is a typical case history, taken from our files. We have deliberately selected a case that occurred more than ten years ago and have altered the names to protect the privacy of the family. Italics have been added to the text:

CONFIDENTIAL

REPORT ON THE McALPINE FAMILY
FROM CASEWORKER

On July 2, I received a call from Mrs. Edward McAlpine regarding a "life and death" matter.

Mrs. McAlpine was seeking protective custody at Bethel Bible Village for her six children, ranging in age from six to fifteen years old. Mrs. McAlpine asserted that her husband, Edward McAlpine, had been engaged in sexual abuse of her daughter, Sandra Trueblood (Mrs. McAlpine's daughter by her first marriage) for the past five years, commencing when the girl was nine. She is now fourteen. The husband, she charged, had also physically abused with his fists and an electrical cord Mrs. McAlpine's oldest son, Norman Trueblood, fifteen, and several of her younger children. (Mrs. McAlpine's first husband, Buford Trueblood, the father of Sandra and Norman, is currently serving a ten-year sentence for armed robbery and assault.)

Mrs. McAlpine first learned of the sexual abuse of her daughter in mid-June of this year, *when her husband informed her of his intention to divorce her and marry his fourteen-year-old stepdaughter*.

A conversation with her daughter confirmed that the girl's stepfather had been physically intimate with her for the past five years. The mother asked her daughter if she would testify against her stepfather if he were prosecuted. The girl, however, refused.

On 6/28, Norman Trueblood informed his mother that his stepfather, while drunk, had told him *he planned to kill both his wife and stepdaughter to prevent them from going to the authorities*. Mrs. McAlpine immediately called the sheriff's department and subsequently filed a charge of aggravated sexual assault against her husband.

On 6/29, Edward McAlpine was arrested at his job and incarcerated in the county jail. (McAlpine had previously been jailed for drunkenness, burglary, and breaking and entering.) Mrs. McAlpine is extremely fearful that her husband will make bond and carry out his threat against her life and that of her daughter.

Our investigation of the McAlpine home, a shabby three-room bungalow, revealed there was no toilet or working bathtub. Dirty clothing was strewn about the front room and bedroom. Dead flies were on and around food left standing on a small kitchen table. Spoiled milk and

> other food was found in the refrigerator; the only edible food in the house was half a box of rice.
>
> The children were unkempt and malnourished. The youngest child had no available diapers and had diarrhea. He was wearing one of the older boy's T-shirts, which was stained with urine and feces.
>
> Our investigators found several rifles and a handgun in the house.
>
> Our investigation has determined that in her present distraught condition, Mrs. McAlpine is unable to care for the children. A petition was filed with the juvenile court on July 10. The judge has recommended that all six McAlpine children be admitted to preplacement at Bethel Bible Village.

The report concludes with the names and ages of the six children and their condition, which was characterized by such phrases as "appears frightened . . . malnourished . . . sexually abused . . . possibly retarded . . . stutters . . . carefree but malnourished . . . needs counseling . . . physically and emotionally abused," and so on.

Sandra Trueblood had a pretty face and dark hair, but she was thin and pale, with the washed-out, pinched look of the poor. At fourteen, she affected a bold manner, imagining herself a man killer. Tragically, her exaggerated view of herself was not all childish fancy. Her stepfather's sexual attentions had introduced and then reinforced these inappropriate ideas. Just before being admitted to Bethel, Sandra had taken up with a truck driver, a man of thirty-two! With her stepfather and her "boyfriend" vying for her affections, what other view could this child have had of herself than that of a temptress?

Sandra was a disturbing influence during her first weeks at Bethel, according to her houseparents, Danny and Benita Davis. She bragged continuously to the other girls in her cottage of her romantic liaisons with "real men." She took to hanging around the baseball field to be seen by the older boys.

Underneath this brazenness was a child starving for attention and genuine love. The only kind of affection she had ever known (if one could call it that) was sexual abuse. The only "love" she had ever known was exploitation of the worst kind; the only intimacy, lustful fondling by grown men. How, at fourteen, could this damaged child be expected to regard men as anything other than potential sexual partners?

In fictional or dramatized depictions of sexual abuse, the victim is usually shown as frightened of her abuser. The truth about real-life abuse (including incest, which we encounter with 80 to 90 percent of our Bethel girls) is far more complicated and shocking.

Sandra Trueblood is a case in point: She actually began to enjoy her stepfather's unfatherly attentions, the sexual appetite having been awakened inappropriately early. She eventually engaged in a form of blackmail against him, enjoying extra privileges as the price of her silence.

The ugly truth shatters our illusion of the totally innocent victim. Yet, if we can suspend our indignation and examine the facts, we see that the truth makes Sandra more a tragic victim, not less. We can see in her distorted ideas of love and romance the full effect of her stepfather's sin against her.

Was this seemingly shameless girl less worthy of our love and understanding? Not at all. On the contrary, we realized that more love and patience would be required because Sandra's wounds were deeper than most; her subconscious self-hatred and despair were greater than we imagined. We knew it would take months, even years, of almost superhuman patience and genuine love by concerned Christian adults at Bethel to repair the terrible damage done to this girl's mind and soul.

My personal involvement with the McAlpine/Trueblood kids was more through Norman than Sandra. Norman had been damaged in ways different from his sister, but he was deeply scarred nonetheless.

On a warm September evening, about three months after the family arrived, I walked into the house for dinner and was greeted by Carolyn, who stood with arms akimbo in the kitchen doorway, a bemused smile on her face.

That look spelled trouble. "Ike, dear," my wife began, "did

you put Uncle Harry [Harry Jackson, our director of family services] up to asking me if Norman could spend the weekend with us?"

I gave her a sheepish look as I went into the bathroom to wash up. "Honey, nobody will take him," I called out as I lathered my hands. Carolyn came and stood in the doorway.

"You couldn't get a sponsor for him?"

"No," I replied. "Word's gotten around about him. He comes off as . . . well, I hate to use the word . . . odd, I suppose."

Once a month we ask Chattanooga families to take one of our children for a weekend. It gives our hardworking houseparents a needed break and gives the children a change of scene and a wholesome experience in a normal home. Many townspeople have responded enthusiastically to our Sponsor Weekends. But Norman Trueblood could have dampened the enthusiasm of a saint.

Norman was not one of our cute little blond tykes who are so easy to love. He had bad habits and a sullen disposition—not Mister Personality by a long shot. And if local people are going to sponsor our Bethel kids as weekend guests, they at least want a little conversation and maybe a smile or two in return for their hospitality. Who can blame them?

Somebody had to take Norman for the weekend, so I had told our caseworker to check with Carolyn.

"What's for dinner, honey?" I asked, giving her a peck on the cheek and heading for the kitchen, from which the delicious smell of roast chicken was emanating.

Carolyn followed me. "Ike, why do *we* always wind up with the tough cases?"

"Because someone has to take them, sweetheart. I can remember all too clearly when no one came to see me at Bonnie Brae."

"You win!" she said. "And you're right . . . the Lord knows somebody has to help this poor lad.

"I heard the other kids pick on him. Ruth Warren [Norman's housemother] says he clams up with the adults but is mouthy with the kids. Makes up all sorts of outlandish stories, so they get on his case. The poor guy's probably starved for attention." With a sigh, she turned back to the stove.

"I think I married an angel!" I said, going up behind her and giving her a squeeze. "And she can cook, too!"

"True on both counts," she said, turning her head and grazing my cheek with her lips. "Now, let me get dinner. Norman will be here soon. Better tell Alan and Brian."

In the early years of our marriage, when our own children demanded a lot of time and attention and she had to mother everyone else's kids, too, Carolyn used to say, "I'm sorry, I just can't give that much of myself. It's so hard to love an unlovely child, who perhaps has a low IQ . . . who may be so scarred he cannot respond. You make so little progress with them. It's heartbreaking."

In the years since coming to Bethel, though, the love of Christ has drawn Carolyn beyond her own likes and dislikes, beyond discouragement, beyond tiredness, beyond her own strength. Because of her willingness, Jesus Christ has given her His love for these hurting children, even the tough cases.

Once Carolyn confided something very precious to me that took me by surprise. "You know, honey," she said, "the Lord helped me overcome something selfish within me, and He used you to do it. Whenever I reach out and hug one of these hurting children, I think, *There wasn't anybody to hug Ike when he was a little boy.* And I want to hug that child . . . because you had no one to comfort you! My heart breaks for the lonely, hurt boy *you* were. So, when I hug one of our Bethel kids, in a way I'm hugging you . . . as you were then. To me, you're all these hurting kids. Does that make sense?"

It made crazy, wonderful sense. And it has given added meaning and depth to our marriage and our commitment to the Lord that we never could have had if we had been living conventional lives for ourselves and our four children. How wonderful and mysterious are the ways of God!

Of course, things didn't seem so wonderful that night when Norman showed up at our door with his bag. It was going to be a long weekend. . . .

Although we had tried to fatten him up in the time he had been with us, Norman, like his sister Sandra, was small for his age. He was almost sixteen but looked fourteen. His mop of unruly black hair made him look even thinner than he was; like his sister, he had a washed-out, unhealthy pallor.

When Carolyn put a motherly arm around his thin shoulder while showing him his room, he stiffened as if avoiding a blow. She pretended not to notice and continued chatting about which dresser was his and did he bring his toothbrush. . . .

Dinner was difficult. Norman barely uttered a word. He sat staring down at his plate, picking at his food. Our girls, Kim and Deb, were polite but silent; our two sons, Alan and Brian, tried talking to him about baseball. Had he caught the Braves game the previous night?

"I hate sports," he replied.

Brain tried again. "Uh . . . how do you like the Warrens for houseparents?"

"They're okay, I suppose."

"Has Uncle Wayne taken you fishing yet?" Alan asked, giving it a try.

"No. I told you, I don't like sports."

"Pass the chicken, please," Deb said nonchalantly. Alan passed the platter, looked at Brian and his sisters, and shrugged.

Having been raised at Bethel, our children were usually at ease with all kinds of kids. We tried to instill in them from the earliest age an understanding that not all boys and girls have loving parents and nice homes. And young as they were at that time, they were learning compassion. But it wasn't always easy.

Norman's lack of responsiveness was eerie and unnerving for our kids. Not once during the meal did he look at any of the children, or at Carolyn or me, for that matter. He kept his head inclined at a peculiar angle, so that all that was visible of his eyes were the black frames of his thick-lensed glasses.

Finally Brian said something about going out to play and asked to be excused. The girls cleared away the dinner plates.

"Are you finished?" Kim asked, looking at Norman's barely

touched dinner. He nodded his head. She looked at her mother, then took the plate away.

Carolyn asked Alan if he had homework—a ploy to make his escape easier. He was away like a shot, leaving Norman between Carolyn and me, staring at the tablecloth.

"If you're hungry later, we'll have pie and milk," Carolyn said, getting up. "Right now, I'll let you two talk," she continued as she headed for the kitchen, where the girls were clattering around.

After a minute or so I said, "Norman, you know Brian and Alan were only trying to be friendly."

"I know,' he replied dully, "but I hate baseball and fishing and stuff."

"That's okay. Did your dad every play ball with you?"

He shook his still-lowered head vigorously. "He *ain't* my daddy. He's my *step*daddy."

"Well, I meant your real father."

"My *real* daddy is living in Knoxville. And he told me he's coming to fetch me. He told me so before I ever come here."

"That would be wonderful, Norman, but your dad isn't in Knoxville," I said gently. "He's in prison. Isn't that so?"

He looked up at me, his eyes flashing. "Well . . . he's going to get out soon. And then he will fetch me!" He looked away.

Silence.

"Norman . . . what were things like . . . I mean at home, with your stepdad? Before you came to Bethel."

"Bad," he replied.

"How did you kids feel about Sandra getting all those extras from him?"

He stared at the tablecloth.

"Your sister did get extra food and privileges you didn't get, didn't she? Am I wrong?"

"No, you're right."

"Do you want to talk about that, Norman? If you don't, that's okay."

After a minute he began to talk. "Once, he took Sandra to Burger King—you know, the one down on the highway. He took her in there and bought her *two* Whoppers and a strawberry shake and fries."

"And what did the rest of you have?"

"Nothing. He told us to wait in the car. But we got out and peeped in the window and saw him and Sandra stuffing their faces."

He spoke clearly and slowly, enunciating his final *g*s as if he were reading.

"That's really unfair!" I said. "Do you . . . hate Sandra for getting all those extras?"

He looked at me again. "No . . . I don't hate my own sister. I hate *him!*"

The boy was able to discern the truth. He knew with a wisdom beyond his fifteen years that his stepfather had instigated this bad situation. Norman was instinctively aware that his sister, for all her arrogance, was a victim.

"Did you know your stepfather was handling your sister?"

"Sure, I knew," he replied almost defiantly, but his head remained lowered. Then, looking at me, he said, "Shoot, I always knew. We have three itty-bitty rooms in our house. You could hear him doing dirty stuff to Sandra. But we always made believe we didn't know."

Looking out the dining room windows, he said in a softer voice, "Mama . . . she didn't know. Maybe she didn't want to know. He did that stuff when Mama was working nights."

He lapsed into silence, staring straight ahead. Then he said in a low, angry voice, "I hope they *never* let him out!"

"Norman," I said, patting his arm, "I know how you feel, because almost the same thing happened to me."

He looked at me with surprise.

"It's true. It was pretty similar to your case, where your stepdad was molesting your sister. In my case, my real daddy was molesting a girl who worked for him—a girl the same age as Sandra. Your stepdad was planning to kill your mom and sister, and my dad killed himself!"

He stared at me, bug-eyed.

"It's true, Norman. My dad committed suicide.

"Now you hate your stepdad. Admitting it is the first step to dealing with it. I might have hated my dad, too, for what he did to that girl and my mother, my brother, and me. But I'm a Christian, and so I've forgiven him, because I know I could do the same thing he did—if I were without faith in Jesus and God."

"I'm never going to forgive him!" He fairly spat the words. "I hope he rots in hell! I really do, Uncle Ike. And I'm not sorry I said it."

"At least you're honest," I said, putting my hand on his shoulder. He flinched. I withdrew my hand. "Someday, Norman, you may be able to forgive him. We can't let the past poison us. Jesus is the One who can help you get a handle on all this anger. . . ."

He looked uncomfortable but I plunged on, wanting to reach this boy, to make him understand.

"Norman, terrible things happen to us. It's a fact of life. And it seems unfair. But God has His hand in there. *The terrible things—no matter how bad they are—don't happen to us apart from God.* He knows all about them! He knows your stepdad beat you with that electrical cord, and He knows the bad things he did to Sandra . . . but you know something wonderful? The Lord can take those very things and turn them around to a good purpose. Can you believe that? It says that right in the Bible. It says, 'And we know that all things work together for good to them that love God . . .' [Romans 8:28 KJV]. And that means the good and the bad."

I could see from the expression in his eyes that he was mulling it over, trying to make sense of it.

"Somehow, God can use all that bad stuff. He can use it to give us spiritual muscles, if we let Him. He can put all our broken pieces back together through His Son, Jesus . . . just as you would glue a broken lamp or vase back together. And somehow, it's even stronger than it was before it got broken!

"And you know something else, Norman? After God puts our pieces back together, we realize that He loves us even more than our parents do. That's right. Sometimes our parents can't love us, because they're all broken, too, and caught by Satan. But God *always* loves us. And He'll never stop loving us, no matter what."

Norman's eyes were fixed on me. I could see the confusion he was feeling, wanting to believe yet not quite able to grasp it all. Had I hit him with too much at once?

"I never really thought about all that stuff," he said after a moment. "Some of it sounds pretty hard to believe, but it kind of makes sense."

I had a feeling he was saying what he thought was expected of him. He wasn't about to vent his real feelings—the hatred and rage, boiling just under the surface. But maybe it was a start.

In the year we had those kids, Sandra calmed down beautifully. Eventually she looked and began acting like a schoolgirl instead of a caricature of a vamp. Her grades improved steadily, and she showed an interest in learning all sorts of things. Her housemother reported that she was a big help with the small children.

Norman, too, made progress. Although he never did get into sports, he occasionally came out of his shell and was able to talk and laugh like the rest of the kids, in spite of his pain. With steady care and attention, he began to stop telling wild stories, as he became a little more secure in our family setting.

When his houseparents, Wayne and Ruth Warren, left Bethel, all the boys in his cottage stood on the steps to see them off.

"I love you, Aunt Ruthie," Norman's little brother, Robert, called out sadly.

"Aunt Ruth . . . Uncle Wayne?" Norman said, suddenly running down the steps to the car.

"Yes, Norman?" Ruth asked.

"I . . . I just want you both to know I really appreciate all you've done. You've been like real parents to us."

"Why, Norman," Ruth replied, hugging him, "I think that's the very nicest thing anybody ever said to me. And I mean that." As Ruth turned to get into the car, there were tears in her eyes.

One day soon after, Mrs. McAlpine visited the children. She asked permission to take them for a little ride. *She never brought them back.*

Eventually, we learned that she drove them to Georgia to live with relatives.

It was sad for us. There was still so much to do for those

children. Yet, we couldn't condemn the mother. Her actions, though misguided, were done out of love for her children.

Were we discouraged? No!

The day I married Carolyn, her mother told me, "Ike, never clutch what you love. Hold it with an open hand, because everything we have is just a gift from God . . . on loan." Mom's words are true. At any time, God could take my wife or my children. And it would be His right. For they are, after all, only "on loan." As Job said, the Lord gives and the Lord takes away.

Our Bethel children, too, are only on loan from God. In most cases, after two or three years of love and Christian nurture, these children go back to their parents, who may be anything but rehabilitated by prison. Some of the parents cannot cope with their own lives, let alone those of their children. So it can be a bad scene all over again.

Yet, for however long these little ones are with us, we and our dedicated houseparents share with them the Good News about Jesus Christ. We teach them God's Word and the principles by which He wants them to live. We try to show them their lives don't have to remain broken, but in Christ they can become the beautiful, whole people God intends them to be.

Because good seed is sown, we know these children will never be the same again. Wherever they go, they will know to whom they can turn in trouble or sorrow. They can say with the Psalmist, "When my father and my mother forsake me, then the Lord will take me up" (Psalms 27:10 KJV). For many of the kids, those words are not mere piety but are literally true.

When Sandra, Norman, and their little brothers and sisters were taken from us and we realized they wouldn't be coming back again, I went to my study and closed the door.

"Father," I prayed, "these are Your children. So now we relinquish them to Your care and protection. Keep them safe in Your love."

Each one of these children is God's special creation. We are to love them for Him. When we do that, we are loving Jesus Himself.

So I pray . . . and the children come, and the children go. And the work goes on. It is the Lord's work. . . .

18. Kids Under Construction

And whoever welcomes a little child like this in my name welcomes me.

Matthew 18:5 NIV

The day-to-day care of our Bethel kids is handled by our team of houseparents. They are a loving, positive influence on these hurting kids. For example, there were Alan and Corolee Pier—"Uncle Alan and Aunt Coco" to generations of Bethel kids who grew up under the loving influence of this wonderful couple.

About one hundred children were raised by the Piers, who were childless themselves but found joy and God's purpose for their lives in caring for troubled children.

When a new child would come, knowing how traumatized he or she was, Alan and Corolee would show the newcomer around the house and tell him or her about the creaks in the floor and the drips in the faucets, so the little one wouldn't be afraid in the night.

Still, Corolee once found a little newcomer sitting up in the dark. "Fred, honey, why don't you lie down?" she gently asked.

"I'm too a-scared to lie down, Aunt Coco," he replied.

Tenderly taking him in her arms, she said, "Fred, dear, Uncle Alan's here, I'm here, the angels are here, and God's here, too. And we're all watching over you. So there's nothing to be afraid of, is there?" Reassured by Corolee's words and motherly embrace, little Fred drifted off to sleep.

Three or four times a week after supper, Alan and Corolee would gather their eight children in the living room and Alan would lead the "family" in Bible reading and devotions. Then, at bedtime, Coco would visit each room and repeat this beautiful Old Testament benediction: "The Lord bless thee, and keep thee: The Lord make his face shine upon thee . . ." (Numbers 6:24, 25 KJV). In the morning, she would wake the children with a joyful acclamation: "This is the day the Lord has made; let us rejoice and be glad in it" (Psalms 118:24 NIV).

Corolee and Alan loved those children. They trained and disciplined them like a real mother and father, when their own parents weren't able to. The Piers went so far as to spend their own money to take the children out to dinner or buy them needed clothes or treats. Once they even bought a beautiful white graduation dress for one of their girls because she couldn't afford one.

After a few months (or years) of this kind of Tender Loving Care, a child begins to think, *I don't know what's going on, but somebody here cares about me. I'm loved.*

Barney and Nancy Speicher have been with Bethel for more than twenty years. They came with us in 1967, two years before we moved to our new campus. They had visited friends who were houseparents at our girls' dorm. Barney had a good job in Elkhart, Indiana, their hometown; they had two sons, Randy and Ron, who were six and nine at the time. The Speichers loved their church and had no intention of moving or changing their life-style.

It seemed odd to the Speichers that when they met Carolyn and me, I had asked them so many questions about their family life, their faith, and their values. They didn't know it, but I was thinking they would make great houseparents! They were committed Christians who openly shared their faith, and from their interaction with their sons and our Bethel kids, I saw that they were loving, responsible people.

Two weeks after their visit, when we asked them if they would consider taking care of our boys' dormitory, Barney wasn't surprised at all—he had felt the Lord nudging him in our direction. The Speichers prayed about it and then accepted our offer.

Since Barney had been in the armed forces and was a no-nonsense man, I placed the Speichers in charge of the older boys who needed the discipline and good work habits they had never gotten at home. But in all their years at Bethel, Barney and Nancy's toughest case was not, as one might expect, a sixteen- or seventeen-year-old but a skinny little kid of eleven, whom I'll call Ralph.

We soon found out that handsome, quiet little Ralph was a sociopath, one of those rare individuals in whom the conscience has never developed. He had no concept of right or wrong or of other people's feelings. (His father was a violent man, serving a long prison sentence; his mother was emotionally unstable and unable to cope.)

On Ralph's first day in the Hixson school system, the teacher called Barney about his disruptive behavior. He refused to do his work, swore at the teacher, and was pushing the smaller children around.

If any kid ever needed a spanking, it was Ralph! When he came home from school, he and Barney had a talk about the need for rules and cooperation.

In many cases a good spanking has a beneficial effect, or at least lets a disruptive child know who is in charge. But in Ralph's case it never did any good. He continued to bully the other kids, sass his teachers, and defy Barney.

Things came to a head one day when the Speichers were on vacation. Ralph stole a rifle and bullets belonging to Bethel. (They were kept in two separate areas under lock and key, for safety.) He sneaked out to the woods with several other kids. A shot rang out and one of the boys dropped. The bullet went right through him and pierced an artery in his lung. The frightened boys carried him back to his cottage. We rushed him to the hospital, where a doctor told us if we had been three minutes later he would have been dead.

Ralph was scared and insisted he was sorry, but his eyes never lost their placid, faraway look. He swore the shooting was an accident.

A short while later, Ralph went back to Chicago to spend the Christmas holidays with his mother. She saw such a big improvement in him that she wanted him to stay. We disagreed, but his mother won out. After returning home, Ralph quickly went from bad to worse and ultimately wound up in prison.

Several years ago, Ralph was out on parole and visited Bethel. His boyish look had been replaced by a dangerous one, but Barney and Nancy welcomed the lost sheep. Before he left, Ralph told the Speichers, "I really messed up good. I should have listened to you when I had the chance. Shoot, I've been in and out of so many jails . . . well, it's too late to cry over spilled milk."

"Ralph, dear," Nancy said, "you're still a young man. *With God, it's never to late."*

We have to believe that at Bethel . . . it's never too late for our kids, even when they've lost their way. We believe in miracles, and we operate on the principle Jesus taught us, of second, third, and fourth chances—up to and beyond seventy times seven. Ralph hasn't used up nearly that many chances. And if Barney and Nancy and the rest of us keep loving Ralph, he may just make it.

Floyd and Deborah Richardson have been at Bethel since 1980. They were Bethel's first black houseparents. They have two children of their own, as well as their "family" of six children at Hipp Cottage. (We recently reduced the number of children from eight to six in a cottage.)

Of all the children the Richardsons cared for in the time they've been with us, it is the Morris family they best remember: Rodney, Mae, Cora, and Elizabeth.

Floyd remembers ten-year-old Rodney as particularly bright, clearly college material, with loads of intellectual curiosity. The first month Rodney was at Bethel he examined every book in the place. He would come home from school each day all excited, wanting to talk about nuclear physics, of all things.

"Uncle Floyd, did you know that the atom is just like a teeny-tiny universe? Teacher told us! The nucleus is the sun and all the electrons—"

"My goodness, Rodney!" Floyd would interrupt, laughing. "Let's talk about baseball or football . . . something I can understand!"

One day the caseworker came without any prior notice and announced the children were going to court that day.

"Aunt Deborah . . . Uncle Floyd," Rodney said, his lower lip trembling. "I don't want to go! I want to stay with you!"

"Don't worry, son," Floyd reassured him, "it's only for a couple of hours. . . ."

The children never came back. The following day, the caseworker returned to pick up their belongings. They had been placed with relatives.

Six years later, a Bethel alumnus visited the Richardsons with three girls. . . the Morris girls, now grown-up teenagers.

Deborah and Floyd just fell all over those kids. They had finally come back to Chattanooga to live with their mother.

"What's Rodney doing now?" Floyd asked.

"He's in college," Elizabeth replied. "He's right outside."

"Well, get him in here," Floyd insisted.

Rodney was now a gangling but handsome young man. He sheepishly took Floyd's hand.

"What's the problem, son? You don't care about Aunt Deborah and me anymore?"

"Yeah . . . I do."

"Pshaw!" said Elizabeth. "All he ever talks about is you two and Bethel!"

They visited awhile, and just before they left, Rodney said, "I do miss you all. If I weren't in college . . . I wish I still lived with you." Then he paused and, looking right at Floyd, blurted out, "Why did you let them take us that time? *Why?*"

"Rodney, there was nothing we could do," Floyd replied. "We had no idea they were planning to take you away that day. It was in the hands of the court . . . the judge. We didn't want it to happen any more than you kids did. Please believe that!"

It was as if a light went on behind Rodney's dark eyes: a light of comprehension and acceptance. Turning to his sisters, he said softly, "Yeah . . . what could they do?"

But he was really telling himself.

We do have our success stories. Take Billy and Liz Hartline: Liz was our first Bethel child to graduate from college. (In fact, Liz was the first in her family to finish high school.) In 1968, she married a minister in the chapel at Old Bethel. Today, she is the mother of four wonderful children.

Her brother Billy's story is a happy one, too. When he was seventeen, we put him to work in the Bethel print shop. Because of the training he received, he was able to get a good job in the printing department of a life insurance company after he graduated from high school.

In 1981, when Billy came to Bethel for the annual reunion, he heard we needed a printer and asked if I would consider him for the job. Would I! I had been praying about it for seven years.

Today Billy says: "I'm grateful I was given a chance here at Bethel. I was loved and cared for by God-fearing people; I learned discipline and decency. Most important, I heard about the love of Christ—and saw it lived—every day at Bethel. And so, in the end, I came to believe. . . ."

Another Bethel child, Devorah, who is now grown, shared her story with us. Although she was never sexually abused, her life was a nightmare of domestic violence. Her stepfather would batter her mother, and when things got too violent, it was Devorah's "job" to call the police.

Here is part of Devorah's story in her own words:

> Finally, one of my mother's friends contacted Bethel. Even though I was a big girl, I was crying when I got here. But when they showed me through the cottages, I saw how nice it was—so clean and cheerful, with two girls to a room and each with their own pretty things, like stuffed toys and pictures. I thought I might like it. At Bethel, I found the care and stability I had been missing . . . and love. Within six months I accepted Jesus as my Savior.
>
> That was four years ago. I'm now attending Columbia Bible College and feel called to the mission field.
>
> If it weren't for Bethel, I don't know where I'd be today—probably on the streets. I wouldn't ever have had a real home. I wouldn't be a Christian. . . .
>
> Through Christian pyschological counseling, I'm learning to face the anger I feel toward Mom. That's the first step toward forgiveness. But it takes time to work through things.
>
> Last Christmas, I visited and she and Tommy were drinking and fighting again. She vomited into her coat. I came back to Bethel early. I try to pray for them. . . .

Two months after Devorah was interviewed for this book, her mother committed suicide. She left Devorah a note. In it she apologized for not having been a better mother, and for what she was about to do, but the pain of living was too great. The last line read: "Devorah, honey, always remember that I love you. . . ."

19. My Flesh and Blood

Train up a child in the way he should go: and when he is old, he will not depart from it.

Proverbs 22:6 KJV

For good or ill, the lives of a man's children are shaped by his own. " '. . .The fathers have eaten sour grapes, and the children's teeth are set on edge' " (Jeremiah 31:29 NIV). Through nature—or nurture—the child resembles his or her parent. Yet the child is not, nor should he be, a carbon copy of the parent. Two traits, conformity and independence, were mixed in our children, as they are in every man's children.

Actually, we had two and two: two independent and two conformable. Kim, our firstborn, and Alan, our youngest, were the strong-willed ones. Deb and Brian were quieter and more compliant. All four are intelligent and articulate. Mealtimes at our house were always lively, sometimes verging on chaotic. All six of us are extroverts and would fight for the floor.

Kim, our firstborn, was the colicky baby. Add to that our inexperience as parents, and you get a rather insecure child.

Perhaps it is significant that Kim's earliest childhood memory is carrying the barefoot little Deb across a road. That's been a metaphor for Kim's life—trying to carry her brothers and sister.

In her record book, Carolyn noted that Kim, from the age of two, imitated her in caring for the other children, acting as if they were her babies.

Deb was a quieter child than her older sister. Her childhood memories seem happier than Kim's, or at least her attitude seems to have been one of peaceful acceptance of things as they were.

Brian and Alan seem to have repeated the pattern established by their older sisters—but in reverse. Brian, the older, is a quiet, deep thinker and devout son, the first of our children to prepare to go into full-time Christian service. His brother, Alan, like Kim, is high-strung, questioning, and independent. But God gifted Alan with a special eye for beauty and creativity, even as a very young child. Today, Alan is a big, handsome, spirited, multitalented young man who will probably embark on a career in the arts.

All four of our children accepted the Lord at a young age. Right from the start, Debbie and Brian had a special love for God, while Kim and Alan had to test and explore the idea of God before committing themselves.

In spite of their differences in temperament, our children all get along and love one another, and are equally loved and valued by their mother and me.

Growing up at Mountain Haven Home and then at Bethel was fun in many ways for our children. They were surrounded by loving Christian adults, and they never lacked for playmates among the staff children and residents of the homes. Living on campus, they never had to dodge traffic in their games; they always had playgrounds and lawns, fields and woods, and, at New Bethel, even a creek for swimming, fishing, and canoeing.

However, our children had some special problems growing up at Bethel, not all of which we were fully aware at the time. For instance, Kim felt she would have given anything to live in a "normal" house, on a "normal" street in town, with a father who had a "normal" job, rather than grow up on a campus with a gang of other kids and a father who didn't go downtown to work, as her classmates' fathers did.

And, just as their Uncle Al had hated the old blue Bonnie Brae bus because it wasn't yellow like the other buses, so Kim and Alan hated our yellow bus because it had the name BETHEL BIBLE VILLAGE emblazoned on the side, which set them apart and labeled them as "different."

What's more, they even felt "different" living at Bethel. "Hey," a friend asked Kim one day, "I saw you with some Bethel kids on their playground. Do you know them?"

"Oh, well . . . yeah," Kim replied, I, uh . . . live *near* Bethel."

Our other two, Debbie and Brian, were more secure and didn't have as difficult an adjustment as Kim and Alan.

However, our children regarded the Bethel kids as their friends. "They were our buddies," Brian says, "just like any kids in a neighborhood."

But some of our children's experiences weren't so typical, or happy. For one thing, because they were the children of the director, people tended to watch them more and to regard them more critically.

At times, my children felt I had a better understanding of the Bethel kids than I had of them. There was understandable but unspoken resentment over this.

Actually, I spent a great deal of what we now call "quality time" with my children. At five o'clock I would leave my office and walk one hundred yards to our home.

God was holding me more responsible for my own children than for all the other children at Bethel. When I came home, I changed roles. I was no longer the executive director of Bethel; I was a husband and father. The Lord showed me early on that before anything—the newspaper, television, meetings—my children needed my attention. I played with them, worked with them, studied with them, and prayed with them.

Yet, I did expect more from our children because they were "privileged" in the sense they had a stable home life and two loving, caring parents. I made it a rule, as much as possible, to treat our children no differently from the way I treated the Bethel children. I'm afraid, though, that this led to some resentment from our brood.

If our children chafed at my way of doing things, they had even more trouble with some of the Bethel kids who, in spite of my attempts to foster equality, were envious of the Keay children because they had a home and parents. Though the Bethel kids liked Carolyn and me, there were instances when they would bad-mouth us to our children just to hurt them and to diminish us in their eyes—because their own parents were in prison or were alcoholics, abusers, addicts, and they were so desperately unhappy about it. Emotionally speaking, the Bethel kids were like cold, hungry children with their noses pressed to the glass of a cheerfully lit candy shop. The name-calling and meanness were futile ways to even the score.

In retrospect, I now realize, to my sorrow and regret, that our children needed more understanding from me. I had plenty of compassion for our Bethel children, but my own four needed compassion, too. As children, they weren't mature enough to comprehend the damage done to the Bethel children so they could make allowances for their misbehavior.

In short, I was bending over backward to accommodate those broken Bethel kids, sometimes, I fear, at my own children's expense.

I was tough on my children in other ways. The legacy of my years at Bonnie Brae and growing up during World War II was organization and discipline. I wanted to pass this valuable training along to my children. If dinner was at five o'clock, then I wanted them washed up and at the table at five. If bedtime was at nine, that meant nine.

Carolyn was different. Getting someplace on time wasn't that important to her. Our differing views on discipline and training was one of our biggest difficulties in marriage. As in many families I, the father, gave our kids external behavioral disciplines and instilled in them a moral code of Christian ethics. Their mother gave them a listening ear and understanding and communicated with them at a feeling level.

The Bethel children seldom revealed the horrible, traumatic things they had seen and experienced. This was, no doubt, partly out of shame and partly because they didn't really know all the sordid facts. If they knew the facts, they were so painful the children suppressed them and tended to live in a fantasy world, so they could cope with the trauma.

As our children got older, we began to fill them in on some of the case histories—particularly when they were having trouble with one of the kids. For instance, we shared with Brian the story of one of his friends—how his mother had shot his father during a drunken family dispute, and this boy had heard it all and saw his father dying on the floor in his own blood. Learning this gave Brian greater empathy for this young friend and admiration for his courage in getting on with his life. I am proud to say that all of our children have grown up with a deep sense of compassion for other people.

I don't want to give the impression that our children's lives were hard and joyless. We had a lot of fun and family times, which were always lively. After dinner each night when the dishes were cleared away, we had family devotions. We would pray and I would read from the Bible and lead a discussion of what the passage meant. On Sundays we often lingered for hours after the meal, sharing and discussing different topics.

But there was a cloud in our blue skies. Throughout our first nine years together, Carolyn remained virtually as strong-willed and independent as the day I met her. She was also as disorganized and inconsistent as I was overorganized and superconsistent. To my way of thinking, she wasn't ever quite as submissive as a Christian wife should be.

In 1967 we both attended a Christian conference in St. Petersburg, Florida, with Dr. Henry Brandt, the noted Christian psychologist. I was thinking, *Maybe he can set Carolyn straight.* I felt sure she was the one with the problem. Unknown to me, Carolyn was thinking, *Maybe this Dr. Brandt can help my husband.* (You can see how mature we both were!)

Dr. Brandt discussed the three words in Paul's salutations: *grace, peace, and mercy.* He asked, "Are you more gracious now than you were last year?"

Regarding the word *peace* Dr. Brandt said, "God's peace comes directly from Him to you. It doesn't come to your spouse first and then to you. Therefore, your peace should not be dependent on what any human being does or does not do to you. No one can take your peace from you and make you angry."

I said to myself, *That's ridiculous! Carolyn upsets me when she does certain things . . . so do the children.*

"Let me explain," he was saying. "If I take this balloon and fill it with water and poke a hole in it, water comes out. If we are filled with anger and hostility and someone 'pokes' us or rubs us the wrong way, that anger comes out of us. But they didn't make us that way. They only brought out of us what was in us."

When Dr. Brandt finished speaking, I felt as if he had riddled me with a machine gun! Until that moment, I had never seen myself as a bad guy. After all, I was a committed Christian. My heart's desire was to please God. But now I realized that I had been guilty of anger, self-righteousness, and pride.

I was shocked that I had been so blind to my own faults. I shared this with Carolyn. She told me the message had hit home with her, too.

We returned home. We had Dr. Brandt's theory; now we had to put it into practice.

One of our alumni, who had left Bethel at fourteen and had wound up in jail, was being released. He was now seventeen and had no place to go. After praying about it, I felt strongly that we ought to let him stay with us.

When I told Carolyn, she announced, "Honey, he is *not* coming into our home."

Ralph had lived with us now and then while he was at Bethel, and he was a terror. From a purely human viewpoint, no woman would want Ralph in her house with her children.

Finally, the day I was going to pick up Ralph at the bus station, she went with me to the door and said solemnly, "I will not be here when you come back. *I am leaving.*"

"Sweetheart," I replied, "you *will* be here when I come back because God gave you to me, and you are my wife." With that, I walked out the door.

Carolyn ran to our room and threw herself on the bed. "Lord," she prayed, "I am so angry at Ike! I could just walk out and leave him . . . but I can't leave the children!"

She was beside herself with anger, but the Holy Spirit began working. "Lord," she said, "the real problem is that I don't have Your love for this boy! I confess to You my anger. Will You please take my anger, Lord . . . and give me Your love for Ralph?"

I came back forty-five minutes later, not knowing what to

expect. We walked through the door and Carolyn was there, greeting us both with a big smile and a hug. I was shocked. God had transformed my wife in forty-five minutes! She did indeed have God's love for that boy.

That's the story of how Dr. Brandt's powerful Christian message changed my wife. But what of me—the man who thought he didn't have too many problems? Well, the acid test of my openness to change was about to occur.

20. Feelings

O Lord, thou hast searched me, and known me. Thou knowest my downsitting and mine uprising, thou understandest my thought afar off.

Psalms 139:1,2 KJV

How can I describe what I was like when I stopped feeling? When I was given something at Bonnie Brae, I would say thank you. But I didn't *feel* thankful; I was merely giving the appropriate response.

When I became a Christian at twenty-one, I had faith in His promises; I was obedient to Him and loyal. But did I *love* Him? Can a man love if he doesn't feel? Everything was up in my head—my computer—not in my heart.

I never consciously felt anger; I would admit to being "upset" over crises, and when my children misbehaved I might be "firm" but never "angry." Anger was a fearsome, forbidden feeling I never consciously experienced.

A few months after Carolyn's dramatic about-face in her attitude toward Ralph, another crisis occurred that put me to the test.

One night we were having chicken potpies for supper. Carolyn was taking them, delicious and piping hot, from the oven and bringing them to the table with tongs.

Suddenly a hot pie slipped from the tongs and fell onto ten-year-old Brian's arm and leg. He screamed in agony as the scalding gravy hit him. Instinctively, I grabbed him, swept the gravy off with my hand, and tore his shirt from his back and arm. Picking him up, I rushed into the bathroom, ripping off his pants as I ran. I turned on the cold water and plunged his burned arm under it while splashing it on his leg. The skin was angry red and already blistering.

The other children sat at the table in shocked silence. They could see it in me . . . *anger.* It was boiling up, as hot and wicked as the stuff that had scalded my little son. *I was angry* that my wife had been so careless. I loved my children so much I did not want them hurt.

Carolyn came to the bathroom door, her face a shocked white mask. Turning to her, my voice brimming with contempt, I said, "You . . . get out of here!" There she was, a hurting mother who willingly would have died before seeing one of her children in pain. She had burned her son by mistake . . . an accident. But I had no sympathy for her. All I could think and feel was, *You're the person who was careless and now he's hurting! Stay out of my way. It's your fault!*

I was comforting and soothing my son, but I was totally insensitive to his brokenhearted mother.

Suddenly, it hit me: *I was angry because anger was there in my heart, just as Dr. Brandt had said!*

I felt so terrible for Carolyn. I walked out of the bathroom with Brian and said to her, "Sweetheart . . . I'm sorry! I was angry. Will you please forgive me? I know it was an accident!"

There were tears in Carolyn's eyes as she brushed past me and embraced our son. "I'm so sorry, Brian. I didn't mean to burn you."

"I know you didn't, Mom," he said. "I'll be okay."

Brian eventually healed but still carries the scars.

I healed a bit, too, starting then. And I also have scars, though mine are invisible. . . .

The years were passing. Our four children were entering their teens. Since we're all committed Christians, there were many questionable activities indulged in by other teens that were off-limits to our kids.

We made up for this somewhat restricted social life by going out of our way to have special fun events for our children. For instance, we always cut down our own Christmas trees and made a party of it. And at bedtime, when the boys would have friends over to sleep, I would tell them ghost stories, making them up as I went along. Those boys loved being scared half to death!

But usually, I would lie down on the bed with the boys with my arms around them, and we would talk about their day. Then we would close in prayer.

Our favorite family pastime by far was throwing elaborate parties. They were legendary. Only recently one of Deb's friends recalled, "The Keays gave the *best* parties around!"

For Kim's Sweet Sixteen celebration, we had a costume party in the barn to which everyone came as eighteenth-century country folk. Carolyn made fancy costumes for the girls, with bodices and long skirts.

While our kids were growing up, we had eight or nine different children living in our house at various times. Our place was always filled with people and laughter and activity. Of course, some of those Bethel children had heavy problems and weren't always fun.

One night, one of our Bethel girls who was desperately unhappy threatened to kill herself when Kim and Deb (who were then in their teens) were home with her alone. The girl was actually holding a knife to her throat. Our girls pleaded with her, but she swore she would do it. Finally Deb said, "Phyllis . . . Jesus doesn't want you to kill yourself! He wants you to be alive and happy!" The mention of Jesus got through to her. She put the knife down. . . .

Those of us in child-care work are always trying to improve ourselves through studying, going to seminars, and so forth. In 1974 Carolyn and I, along with houseparents Bob and Jewel McFarland and another couple, attended group counseling sessions with Bethel's Christian counselor, Dr. Bob, who had been working with our Bethel kids for five or six years. None of us were having any serious marital problems; we just wanted additional insight into our individual personalities.

I know there are Christians who have no use for counselors or psychologists at all. But it is foolish for Christians to ignore God-given help that is at hand from biblically oriented counselors who are specialists in the human psyche and are being led and directed by the Holy Spirit.

When people are lost and damaged to the extent of some of our Bethel kids, for example, Christian counseling by laymen is not enough. Deeply hurt people need expert help from Christian professionals.

Wounded parents tend to pass their brokenness on to their children. It was true in our family. All four of my children were scarred somewhat by my childhood legacy. If only I had known how damaged I was before I married Carolyn! I desperately needed counseling to restore my brokenness. For most of my life I have been emotionally handicapped, hurting my dear wife and precious children. And I didn't know it. We were all confused. Something was wrong but none of us knew what it was.

The point is this: *There was no way I could go through all that trauma in my childhood and not come out deeply scarred.* To just about everyone I appeared very normal. And yet, deep inside, I was only half a person. My father's self-centeredness had cost me dearly and, in turn, seriously affected my family.

But how I praise God that He (and others) can bring healing and wholeness to hurting adults and children. I feel because of the insights we've all gained, my children will actually be stronger in the long run and more equipped to understand themselves and help others.

I've digressed from my story, which in itself is a good illustration of Christian therapy in action. That night everyone took turns telling his or her story, and then Dr. Bob asked us questions that had a way of cutting through all the evasions and forcing the person in the "hot seat" to face the uncomfortable truths he or she had been evading.

In those sessions, Dr. Bob gave each one of us golden nuggets of insight and truth about ourselves. But it was painful. People were breaking down, weeping as they faced the truth.

Then it was my turn. When I had finished my story, Dr. Bob asked me, "Ike . . . what are you feeling?"

"What do you mean, what am I feeling?" I responded.

"Do you have a tightness in your throat . . . maybe a knot in your stomach or an ache in your neck?"

"No . . . am I supposed to?"

"Yes, you're 'supposed to,' " he replied. "Have you seen all these other people crying over their stories? Do you see them crying over yours right now?"

"Yes."

"You don't feel any of that?"

"No." But I was beginning to be uncomfortable.

"Ike," he said, "when did you stop . . . *feeling?*"

"What do you mean, 'stopped feeling'?"

"You don't feel much of anything, do you? You haven't for years, have you?"

Suddenly a line from a speech I had been giving in churches for over ten years, about our Bethel ministry, flashed through my mind: *These kids are hurt so deeply they stop feeling.*

Was that what Dr. Bob had said? *No, no . . . that line wasn't about me . . . it was about our Bethel kids. . . .*

I was stunned. It couldn't be true! *I have such tremendous empathy for hurting people. I'm a hugger and a kisser.*

Now, in a rush, the curtain parted and I saw the truth: I had been talking about the hurting Bethel kids not being able to feel . . . but it was me all the time. . . .

"Ike . . . you stopped feeling way back," Dr. Bob said gently. "Why do you think you stopped feeling?"

"Because I was taken away from my mother and left with a bunch of strangers," I heard myself saying. "The pain was so awful . . . it hurt so much, I began dying that day."

Since that night in 1974, I have been very slowly getting in touch with my long-lost feelings. It isn't easy. I still say, "*We* love you," to my children, meaning their mother and I. I find it so hard to say, "*I* love you." My progress has been an on-again, off-again thing, an uphill struggle.

Christmas 1984, ten years after that breakthrough, Brian was home from Capernwray Bible College in England. He tried talking to me about feelings. When I was unresponsive, he vowed to himself that he wouldn't broach the subject again. "My dad is just not capable of responding at a feeling level."

But the next year, Christmas 1985, Carolyn, Brian, and I were sitting at the kitchen table at midnight. Brian decided he would take another chance with me. I'm so glad he felt I was worth it.

"Dad," he began, "there's a deep side of me that wants to see a deep side of you. I know you have a deep side in there."

He was looking at me intently.

"Dad . . . I love you."

I looked at him and said, "I know that, Brian,"

I could feel his eyes on me. "Dad," he said again with a soft intensity, "I really *love* you!"

"You don't have to tell me that, Brian. I know you love me."

"*But Dad . . . I really love you!*" His eyes were intense. Tears were on his cheeks. I was feeling (*really* feeling) uncomfortable. I could hardly stand the heat. I suddenly realized I could turn it off, or I could feel the feeling. I chose to stay with him.

Now tears were in my eyes, too. I looked at my son and felt his love for me; it was tender, human, and warm.

After a moment, he said, "Dad, you felt something then, didn't you?"

"Yes," I replied, "I did."

It was another breakthrough and one of the most beautiful experiences of our lives.

Another great experience was Brian's wedding to his lovely Annie. I cried uncontrollably for five or ten minutes. That's beautiful for me.

I pray about feeling my feelings. I work at it, though never as conscientiously as I should. I know that, with patience, the Lord will eventually restore my feelings and make me a whole person again.

A couple of years ago, Carolyn and I found ourselves rattling around in the house. We had just put thirty-four people from Ireland, who had been on a work team at Bethel, on a bus bound for Nashville. Now we were suddenly alone. Our home, which for so many years had rung with discussions and laughter, tears and life, was quiet as a tomb. Alan, our youngest, had just left to live in California.

I sat down on the sofa in the family room to relax. My eyes wandered to a shelf where so many of our kids' things were: pictures, tapes of Kim's wedding, books, games, a ceramic duck Alan had made. Suddenly, it hit me: After twenty-nine years of raising children, we were alone. Our whole married life had centered around our children, and now they were gone.

Other than God Himself and my dear wife, my children were the most important things in my life. To me, raising children was the greatest job in the world. And now my job was over.

An overwhelming sense of loss grabbed me. I knew I could click off the uncomfortable feeling as easily as I could turn off a radio.

No, I said to myself, *I'm not going to turn it off. I'm going to let it come. I'm going to feel it all . . . the absence of my dear children . . . the pain, the loss. . . .*

And I began to cry. I cried and cried. Carolyn came into the room and saw me weeping, openly, unashamedly. And she was so touched that I could be crying—feeling my feelings—that she began to cry, too.

She came and sat down on the couch beside me, and we put our arms around each other and cried . . . together.

Afterword

Children of Joy

O thou afflicted, tossed with tempest, and not comforted, behold, I will lay thy stones with fair colors, and lay thy foundations with sapphires. . . .

And all thy children shall be taught of the Lord; and great shall be the peace of thy children.

Isaiah 54:11, 13 KJV

The job was finished. Carolyn and I had few regrets. We had invested our lives in our children and they, in turn, had enriched our lives beyond measure. There was a sense of deep satisfaction.

We had spent a great deal of time with our children, and now the nest was empty. We were ready for a new chapter.

Carolyn and I still love each other deeply. We have worked through most of our problems. We look forward with anticipation to what God has for us next. And now I can devote myself more fully to my second love—the children of Bethel Bible Village.

On the most obvious level, the purpose of Bethel Bible Village is to provide a caring home and a wholesome temporary family for the hurting children of prisoners, until their own homes can be restored. We try to give them much more than shirts on their backs and food in their stomachs.

On a deeper level, however, we are in the business of giving hope to these hurting children: hope in God; hope that there is still some goodness in the world; hope for a better life; hope of heaven.

This great work, begun so many years ago by Brother Hipp, is God's work. It has gone forward and has grown and prospered, but not without much prayer, effort, and constant tending.

The Lord gives us manna for the day. Because we rarely receive more than seventy-five percent of what we need to operate monthly, we have prayed and racked our brains to come up with creative ways of raising funds to keep things going here.

One day in December 1972, I got a call from one of Bethel's regular supporters, Terrell Fugate, a Chattanooga businessman.

"Ike," he said, "you know how much I love golf. Would you mind if we got a little golf tournament together—any money we make on it we'll give you for the kids of Bethel."

I replied, "That sounds like a super idea, Terrell!"

"Maybe we can interest some wealthy benefactor out there—somebody who loves golf—to really get behind Bethel, maybe underwrite your whole budget, so you won't have to scratch around anymore."

Terrell recruited Sam Woolwine, one of the sportswriters at the *Chattanooga News–Free Press*. Sam, in turn, got a friend named Fred Holland interested. So the three of them spearheaded the tournament.

Those men got a group of 150 players, who paid thirty-five dollars each, plus 29 celebrities, to compete. The tournament was held in March 1973 at the Creek's Bend Golf and Country Club.

Among the celebrity athletes that first year were pitcher Bob Turley of the New York Yankees and Steve Sloan, famed Alabama All-American. When the weekend was over, we had netted forty-five hundred dollars, which was fantastic for the first year.

Terrell and his group felt so good about the tournament that they decided to hold it again the following year—but in May, when the weather would be better.

The second year they got Kyle Rote, Jr., and his dad, CBS commentator Kyle Rote, Sr., to participate.

The third year, they asked a celebrity to host the tournament. Country-music star Tom T. Hall agreed to come from Nashville.

It was a wonderful gesture for a star of Hall's stature and drawing power to make himself available for Bethel. That year they changed the name of the tournament to the Tom T. Hall Celebrity Golf Tournament.

Our proceeds that year jumped to eight thousand dollars. The following year the tournament made a quantum leap to a handsome twenty-two thousand dollars in profits, with even more celebrities and bigger crowds.

In February 1978, I was snowed in in Kalamazoo, Michigan, when I got a long-distance call informing me that Tom T. Hall would not be available to host the tournament that year. I was stunned.

"Lord," I prayed, "this has been one of the best things that has ever happened to Bethel. People have heard about us; it's put us on the map. Lord, I can't believe You want me to let this thing die. What do You want me to do?"

Then I got an idea . . . it was a slim chance but worth a try. When I got back to Chattanooga, I called a friend, Nick Boone, who is Pat Boone's brother.

"Nick, do you suppose you could ask Pat if he would help us out, come down for a weekend in May. . . . I know he must get a lot of requests like this, but we're really in a bind. If we could get a star like Pat. . . ."

"Sure, Ike," he replied. "Look, I can't promise anything. Pat's always booked solid. But I'll ask. Let's be in prayer about it."

When Nick explained the situation to Pat Boone, that the tournament was only three months away and the host had canceled, Pat graciously agreed to step in—but only for one year.

Pat didn't know what awaited him in Chattanooga, but I'll let him tell that:

> I really wasn't ready for the welcome. When I got out of the private plane, flown by Bethel board president Ted DeMoss, I was suddenly engulfed by a swarm of beautiful young kids, hugging me and talking to me all at once: "Hi, Uncle Pat!" . . . "Thanks for coming to help us, Uncle Pat!" . . . "Are you a good golfer, Uncle Pat?" . . . "Is Debby coming, Uncle Pat?"
>
> A kindly but authoritative gentleman (Ike Keay) began to gently shepherd them away from me, chuckling as he said, "Come on, kids, let's give Uncle Pat some room! Let him

breathe! We'll take him out to Bethel, and you can ask him questions there."

I wasn't ready for Bethel, either. No one can adequately describe Bethel Bible Village—the grounds and the cottages and the main buildings; the natural Tennessee beauty of trees and gently rolling meadows and the pond. A nearby creek has an "old swimming hole," complete with the rope that allows young Tarzans and Janes to swing off the dock into the creek below. It's a Norman Rockwell cover. I am hard-pressed to convey the overwhelming sense of love and belonging that permeate the whole setting.

We had a sort of picnic that afternoon; then Ike and Carolyn Keay took me into the main assembly hall, a friendly room about the size of two or three garages, where kids got to fire their questions at me. We ended up singing Christian songs in a spontaneous concert. It was so joyous, so "right," so moving, in a hopeful and positive way, that I was stirred deeply.

I picked up a winsome little girl of five or six and sat her on my knee while we listened to the other kids sing. Ike leaned close to my ear—the one away from where the little girl sat—and told me just a little of what she'd been through, how her own father had abused her and offered her for the pleasure of other adult men. "It's really a miracle she'll let you pick her up and that she'll sit on your knee. I thought you'd like to know the progress she's made already."

I was stunned. I wanted to cry. I wanted to hold her close, to take her back home with me. Protect her. I couldn't do any of that, of course, but then I heard Ike saying, "Almost all of these kids have stories like that, and that's why Bethel is here."

Now, suddenly, the sound of their music, the sight of their fresh scrubbed faces—their "joyful countenances"—was almost more than I could take. But I was hooked. Boy, was I hooked!

At a press conference Pat told reporters, "I've been going to prisons for years, working with inmates, but I never once thought, *What happens to their children?* And I just love golf, so what better way to help these children and at the same time enjoy a good game of golf? What a fantastic combination!"

That year, 1978, thanks to Scotty Probosco's efforts, the spectacular was held at a new location, the Rivermont Golf and Country Club in Chattanooga, which was owned by Scotty's friend Russell Mitts. He was helped by tournament director John Reed and later, Bill Buchanan. We had a grand weekend—the most fun ever. People just flocked to see Pat, and we had a great concert. Pat seemed to enjoy himself thoroughly. Then, just before he left, he said to me, "Ike, I'll be coming back again . . . next year."

Pat did come back the next year, and the next. He's been returning to Bethel every year, bringing a host of celebrities with him. In his honor, we renamed the tournament the Pat Boone Bethel Celebrity Spectacular. It is held on the second weekend in May.

In the years since Pat joined us, the spectacular has expanded to include Christian seminars with a family orientation, featuring speakers such as Dale Evans, Ann Kiemel Anderson, Debby Boone, Beverly LaHaye, Zig Ziglar, Dr. Henry Brandt, and Kyle Rote, Jr. (We feel it is important to have spiritual input during this fun-filled weekend.)

Our other big fund-raising event at Bethel has been our annual Country Fair, held each fall. It, too, began in a small way in 1978, when members of the Northgate Chapter of the American Business Women approached us and said they wanted to do something for our Bethel children. They suggested a giant flea market. That first year we called it Good Neighbor Day. In addition to raising money, the event got people out to see our campus, stimulating community interest in Bethel.

Like Topsy, it "just growed" to include arts and crafts, horse rides for the children, games, food stands, and cake sales. We changed the name to the Bethel Country Fair. Two years ago, the fair raised thirty-four thousand badly needed dollars for our Bethel kids.

* * *

The Lord knows how much we still need for Bethel Bible Village. But God depends on people; He inspires Christians to roll up their sleeves and get involved.

I get frustrated at times, dreaming of what we could have at Bethel—what we *will* have one day, Lord willing. The list of improvements we must make to help these children goes on and on. Some things are already on the drawing boards:

Special Learning Center: We planned to start this in 1988, but we didn't have the financial resources. It will be a school for Bethel children with learning disabilities and behavior problems. Public and Christian schools often cannot cope with Bethel's problem kids; they are simply not geared to handle them. "Your children take too much individual attention," they tell us.

Because of the trauma in their young lives, too many of our Bethel children are quitters. Many have attention deficit disorder—they have no ability to concentrate.

We at Bethel must address the problem to help these damaged children get back self-control and self-esteem, so they can regard school as more than a prison sentence.

Gymnasium-Pool-Office-Special Education-Arts Complex: Bethel kids have never had a gymnasium or a swimming pool so they could have an adequate athletic program. Most children's homes have these facilities. Bonnie Brae had them more than fifty years ago.

We have a gymnasium-pool-office-special education-arts complex on the drawing boards. It will be a wonderful building. It will also house an adult-education program to teach people in the community how to be good husbands, wives, and parents, and it will contain a counseling center.

I know how effective sports can be. The excellent athletic program at Bonnie Brae Farm pulled me out of the pits, put me together again, and restored my self-esteem. Our children desperately need a program like that at Bethel.

The schools in the community have coaches and sports programs, *but it takes a Bethel child much longer than other children to learn.* They get discouraged so quickly because all they've ever known is defeat. They have been verbally abused, physically abused, sexually abused. Self-esteem is nonexistent.

Arts, Music, Crafts Program (to be housed in the gymnasium-office complex): We need programs in arts and crafts, painting, voice, piano, and guitar so we can steer kids into areas where they have potential. Then they'll be able to say, "Hey . . . I can do this!" and begin to change that poor self-esteem. It's a long, slow process but critical to their survival. We *must* get started.

In short, we need an all-around program to find the slightest strengths, skills, talents. That will, in turn, help them with academics, and they will begin to feel better about themselves and their abilities. Once we get them functioning academically, we can return them to the regular school system.

If we don't begin to strengthen the self-esteem of these damaged children, they will end up by dropping out and using drugs and alcohol, like some of their parents. *If the cycle of poverty and crime and sin is ever going to be broken, these children have to learn to feel good about themselves.*

Vocational Training: Once we get the gymnasium-pool-office-special education-arts complex constructed, it will free our present administration building, which was originally intended to be our vocational training center. It will finally become that when we can hire instructors and buy (or have donated) the machinery and equipment to give the kids hands-on training.

Vocational training has been the big lack in our Bethel program. Of what use is it to raise children in a loving family environment, only to send them out into the marketplace with no real abilities and skills? How can they make a living? How can they support a family?

With few exceptions, that is what has been happening to too many of our Bethel children over the years. Although a few go on to college, most wind up in unskilled, low-paying jobs. Some repeat the pattern of their parents and turn to liquor, drugs, and crime. The loss of potential and the drain on the community is enormous . . . and sinful.

Most of our kids have psychological handicaps. If we don't

begin to give them marketable skills to make a living, they might never make it. They will wind up on welfare, or in crime like their parents.

Multiunit Residence Building: Also on the drawing boards is a new, multipurpose residence building. Besides containing living quarters for some staff, it will house our volunteers—retired persons, college students, and professors who offer to donate their time and skills to Bethel. Right now we're turning volunteers away, and that just kills me.

This building would also serve as a transition house for some of our eighteen-year-olds who are working off campus but are not yet able to make it on their own. The fact is that some of our kids fall on their faces their first year or so and have no home or parents to turn to. They would come back for a while and live in this unit.

We would use a certain number of the units as a halfway house for some of the more responsive parents of our children when they are released from prison. They would live at Bethel and could be employed on campus. At the same time we would be working with them, helping them to learn what it is to be a real mother or father to their children.

Additional Cottages: We need an additional staff cottage for an athletic director, and we have room for four more cottages—one for boys and three for girls. These would be slightly smaller than our present cottages, since we are dropping the number of children in each from eight to six.

It is an ambitious program, but we are people of faith. Our philosophy is, "Expect great things from God. Attempt great things for God."

Early in this book is the following verse:

> *And we know that in all things God works for the good of those who love him, who have been called according to his purpose.*
>
> Romans 8:28 NIV

All things . . . not *some* things. We glibly say we believe God, but do we honestly believe that every single thing works together for good?

Think about the story of Joseph in the Bible: Joseph was his father's favorite. He was also an obedient son. But he was sold into slavery and later accused of rape and thrown into prison.

Later, after Joseph was vindicated and made the second most powerful man in Egypt, his brothers came seeking food. When they learned that this powerful official was their brother, they were scared to death because of what they had done to him. But he said, ". . .you meant evil against me, but God meant it for good . . ." (Genesis 50:20 NAS).

I think of my own childhood. After all that suffering, today I am the director of Bethel Bible Village, the only home in the United States for the children of prisoners. God took the broken pieces of my life and put it back together. Then He gave me a ministry to hurting children.

The question is this: Does everything work together for good? I leave it to you who have read my story to decide.

The Apostle James said we are to "visit the fatherless and widows in their affliction. . ." (James 1:27 KJV). This has always been the responsibility of God's people.

I know the children of Bethel Bible Village are very dear and precious to our Lord Jesus Christ, and with His powerful, thought-provoking words I close:

> *"Then the righteous will answer Him, saying, 'Lord, when did we see You hungry, and feed You, or thirsty, and give You drink? And when did we see You a stranger, and invite You in, or naked, and clothe You? And when did we see You sick, or in prison, and come to You?' And the King will answer and say to them, 'Truly I say to you, to the extent that you did it to one of these brothers of Mine, even the least of them, you did it to Me.' "*
>
> Matthew 25:37–40 NAS